Xwist Memin Kin
"I Want to go Home"

Memories of Kamloops Residential
School and Joeyaska Ranch

MARY JANE JOE

Tellwell Talent
www.tellwell.ca

ISBN
978-0-2288-5025-0 (Paperback)
978-0-2288-5024-3 (eBook)

Table of Contents

Ntle'kepmx pronunciation:

ł - barred "L" = tl sound.
X – ch as in Bach.
In – means "my" (in jowa – my name)
"i" – is "ee" sound (shi'itm – family)

A TRIBUTE TO:

My late parents Frederick Albert Sterling, Inxwhup and Sophie Sterling née Voght, Tli tletko, and my late grandmother Ya-yeh (Shanny Voght née Antoine)

My resilient great grandparents: Joeyaska and Buelt'ko.
Skaz'a – father: to discipline with affection.
Skix'ze – mother: nurturing hands.
Kz'e, Ya-yeh – grandmother: affectionate.
in shi'i'tm - My relatives who walk alongside me and help me to grow up strong and independent.
Ce'xw mixc – With appreciation.

WRITTEN FOR:
My children Darren and Nadia.
And my grandchildren Juliette, Virgil and Harrison.
My story is your story.

FOREWORD

"I fought for my destiny, fought in the sky. If you
think to shatter me, I dare you to try."

Seepeetza

I was set to publish this book when the Tk'emlups te Secwepmc First
Nation announced that the bodies of 215 Indigenous children were found
buried in a mass grave on the grounds of the former Kamloops Indian
Residential School.

I attended Kamloops Indian Residential School from 1957 to 1969.
After reading the announcement, I struggled with whether or not to
proceed with publication. Some of the vignettes in my memoir suddenly
seemed frivolous in comparison to the gravity of this revelation. In the
end, I forged on.

I dedicate this book to my 215 classmates who never returned home,
and to all the grieving relatives.

Sincerely,
Mary Jane Joe
Musqueam Territory

FAMILY LIFE AT JOEYASKA RANCH

Ye tik sinwenwen! Greetings in the Ntle'kepmx language. My elders always began their story or lesson with these words: *xwi kin spilax hin.* "I will tell you my story."

Injowa Nk'xetko. I am Nk'xetko. My name means cutting deer meat with a sharp knife, piercing the bone and cooking it in water. In essence I am the woman who carries that out and makes delicious food. I am named after Dad's great aunt. This is all we knew about it. Dad gave me that name when I was born in 1950. He then named me Mary Jane at my baptism two months later. That's when the priest registered me with an English name for Catholic and governmental records. I'd heard that priests couldn't spell or pronounce our names. I knew myself mainly as Nk'xetko, and various nicknames along the way. I wondered why Dad chuckled when he spoke to me as Nk'xetko. Years later, I learned its true meaning.

I am the second youngest of seven siblings. We all carried traditional names along with English names and, like our parents who were status Indians and registered as wards of the Canadian government, we all attended residential school. It was the law.

Both of my parents attended school in the early 1900s when beatings and whippings were regularly carried out to enforce learning English. As a result, I heard our language in the home, but no one spoke it directly to us children. My grandmother Ya-yeh didn't speak English at all, nor had she gone to school. When she spoke to us in her natural way, her eyes twinkled behind the spectacles on her nose. Her words sounded kind and gentle, peppered with laughter, whereas the English language sounded strict and harsh.

My first memory is of sitting on the back of my mom's saddle, holding onto side straps as we rode up a trail behind my dad on his horse, JW Baldy. My youngest brother, Austin, was strapped in behind him. We plodded along in the hot sun, the horses huffing and snorting up the gravel trail. We were heading up to Godie Canyon beyond Joeyaska Ranch, our family home. Years later, I asked Mom if this memory was true or imagined.

"Oh yes" she said. "We were heading up the hill to check on the wild raspberries. We used to travel everywhere on horseback."

Berry picking was an important pastime for our family in the summer months. As young children, we learned to fill a basket with berries and do our share to provide fruit for the winter months. Every season meant different foods were ripe and we had to go harvesting. Spring, for example, brought the bitter roots, wild potatoes and thunder mushrooms. As a child I just wanted to play, but Dad was serious when he pressed us to do our part.

Dad inherited a few head of cattle along with a 320-acre plot of land from his mother, Sarah Joeyaska Sterling (Pow tan malks, which means Echo). Sarah's father, known as Joeyaska, was an Okanagan who had lost everything in the Indian conflicts, either the Spokane or the Cayuse Wars in the 1860's in Washington State. He made his way to Douglas Lake where he had relatives and put down roots at Nicola Lake. There he grew hay and raised horses until a European rancher legally displaced him in the 1800s when lands were parcelled up by the government. Joeyaska found himself homeless until he heard about "Preemption," which meant claiming unowned property in blocks of 160 acres called "Homestead." It meant fulfilling strict rules of land ownership including the digging of irrigation ditches, building log homes, barns and corrals, as well as installing fences and clearing fields to plant gardens and hay crops. Joeyaska successfully preempted two homestead properties. Land Commissioner G.M. Sproat issued that to him in 1878. It's been in our family ever since. Joeyaska and his family lived in teepees in summer and pit houses in winter. I'd heard about that history since I was born and saw those rounded depressions on the land.

Dad's father, Charlie Sterling, died in the Spanish flu pandemic in 1918. Prior to that he drove a wagon train delivering dry goods to towns.

He was away from home a lot, which is why Joeyaska and his wife, Martha (Buelt'ko, as we knew of her), cared for Dad until he turned seven. That's when Joeyaska enrolled Dad in a boy's school in New Westminster, BC, for one year, then Dad was sent to St. Mary's Indian Residential School in Mission, BC, for seven years. Dad ran away from St. Mary's in 1910 at age fourteen due to the harsh treatment he received at the hands of the priests. He lived in hiding for two years because priests and police ordered Sarah to send him back to school. Instead, Dad worked as ranch hand at Nicola and Douglas Lakes until he enlisted in World War I. He fought in Europe, was wounded and returned to his home at Joeyaska in 1919. By then his mother was alone. She was glad to see him, and he worked hard to maintain the fields and livestock that were left in his care by his uncles and grandfather. After she lost her log house in a fire, Dad built her a small house with lumber from the mill. I recall how busy he was every day, no matter the season. I clearly recall him feeding cattle in -40°C weather.

As the youngest children, Austin and I were the last ones at home during summer months because our older siblings had gone off to work or to school. There wasn't much to do sometimes, so we liked to follow Dad around as he mended fences, fed the animals and cleared the ditches that watered the hay fields. Dad had a sweat lodge beside a deep ditch among the pine trees. Occasionally, he'd build a fire, heat flat rocks and go inside for a sauna-like steam cleanse. No one explained much to us about this ritual, but we liked hearing the steam hiss when cold water hit the rocks. We later learned the sweat lodge was a sacred space to give thanks and pray for cleansing and purification. A mysterious notion we hoped to join someday. It sounded important.

Our favourite pastime was watching him make horseshoes in the blacksmith shop, a square log building that had once been Uncle Barnes' home.

I felt connected to an uncle and grandfather I'd often heard about but never met. They had put up barns, corrals and houses on this cleared land they had carefully tended 100 years prior. Their strong presence was all around me. Joeyaska owned many horses before he died in 1908. A tame, trained horse was a valuable trade item in the bartering system before money was introduced.

Making horseshoes was a long, drawn-out process. I was feeling impatient one day and asked Dad why he had to do it.

"It's important to protect the horses' feet," he said.

We waited under the horses' bellies and played around their legs. We weren't afraid; we loved those gentle horses. When Dad needed red hot coals for the iron, Austin and I would race to press air through the bellows. I was always struck by the way Dad worked in a careful way in every detail—as though our lives depended on it. One time, Austin stared in wonder as Dad trimmed off a horse hoof, observing that it resembled a giant, shriveled toenail.

Mom milked a cow in the corral nearby. She always got two buckets of milk then made butter. If there was extra milk, cream or butter, we delivered it to our neighbours down the road. They were glad to see us and happy to receive fresh gifts from the milk cow. My parents demonstrated generosity. It was important for them to share whatever they had with others. I liked the taste of fresh milk too. Once when no one was looking, I took a spoon and scooped up some thick cream to my mouth. Austin saw me and warned, "I'm telling!" I tossed the spoon into the dishpan and took off.

Mom kept busy baking bread, doing laundry, preserving fruit and berries, weeding the garden in the summer and helping with the haying. I rarely saw my parents sit down, except for meals. I often wondered where my older siblings were and later learned they were working for wages elsewhere. Dad never paid us for working on the ranch; instead, he pressed us to go to college, get work and make a life for ourselves. I remember my home life as relaxed and routine. Our parents made us feel safe and provided a home where I felt nurtured.

We had to help pack wood and ensure the water buckets were filled. Our great-grandfather had dug a deep well for fresh drinking water. Each day, much water was used for cooking and washing, and every one of us had to fetch water to meet the need. Overflow from the well trickled into a nearby pond. In the summer, the pond was fun to play in when the adults weren't looking, but far too muddy for anyone's liking. The livestock didn't mind drinking pond water where the runoff flowed sparkling and clear and tiny green watercress glistened.

Springtime meant preparing fields for the new crop of hay. I remember Dad hitching up the team of horses to brush harrow all the fields. After that, he hitched up a plow to one of the horses to make a large garden for vegetables and potatoes in one of the upper fields. It took almost one full day to turn over the black soil into neat rows ready for planting seeds. Sometimes I liked to follow behind Dad while he plowed. I picked up earthworms and put them in my pockets to give to the chickens later. On laundry day, Mom cleared dried earthworms from my pockets, shaking her head at me as she fed them to the chickens.

The gas-powered washing machine was noisy and did a good job of getting our clothes and sheets clean. I liked how fresh the wind made the laundry on the clothesline smell. As a toddler, I burned the skin above my knee while playing too close to the washing machine's hot exhaust hose. That scar reminded me to keep away from motors and to listen to my parents' warnings.

One summer day in early July, I saw Mom and Ya-yeh put on their big straw hats and head up to the garden to do the weeding. They sat on gunny sacks for hours pulling out weeds. There was no one in the house, so Austin and I prepared to join them. He wore swimming trunks and a beaded pendant. He carried a long stick that he called his spear.

"Are you the man known as Chief Beards?" I asked him.

I had meant to say Chief Beads, but he had already taken offence. Austin took offense at anything and everything I said or did.

"I am not Chief Beards!" he hollered, chasing me through the field.

His spear disrupted bees on the alfalfa blossoms, and a swarm chased him, stinging his head and body as he ran back to the house. Later, after he had regrouped, he met us in the garden wearing a rolled-up towel around his head. Mom told me not to say a word, implying that I'd already caused enough trouble. I kept quiet the whole afternoon, pulling weeds.

Mid-July meant the haying season began after any danger of rain had passed. Damp hay could ruin the crop with mold. Dad harnessed up his two work horses to the mowing machine and cut hay in the main fields. For days he worked from early morning until supper time, stopping only briefly for lunch, until the job was done. The pungent, damp smell of freshly cut hay, mostly sweet alfalfa, reminded us it was the middle of summer. We looked at the sky often during those times, hoping the rains would hold off. It was a relief when the hay got put up without fear of rain. Sometimes rabbits that lived in the fields were mowed down, which resulted in a tasty meal at supper. We were considered Catholic, so we generally didn't eat meat on Fridays. However, one Friday we forgot and were enjoying fried rabbit when someone spoke up. We ruminated on whether we would go to hell for our misstep until Mom explained that it was an honest mistake and we'd be forgiven. Still, we all ate in silence after that.

After the hay was cut, it had to dry out for a few days before raking could begin. That meant a trip to the Coldwater River for an afternoon of swimming. Mom packed a picnic lunch, and we splashed and yelled to our hearts content.

After the hay dried in the hot sun, Dad harnessed up the horses once again—this time to pull a raking machine. He sat on a seat in the middle of two large wheels that propelled large rakes that looked like giant curved fingers. This gathered the hay into neat rows. It was slow work, but he managed well, steering with the reins, making the horses work hard. Sometimes it was my job to bring the horses to the pond to drink after they were set loose. It was thirsty work. Otherwise, Austin and I stayed far from all moving machinery. We found things to do close to the house, like play a game of marbles or make mud pies at the pond.

After the hay dried, everyone swung into action. If my older siblings worked nearby, they came home to help. They grabbed straw hats and pitchforks and headed out to the fields. My family pitched hay into piles in the hot sun, faces sweaty, until days later when the neat stooks dotted the fields. My job was to bring a jug of cold water for everyone to enjoy a refreshing drink.

The sloop, or hay wagon, came out after that. Again, it was all hands on deck. If my siblings couldn't make it, Dad paid people to help because the work had to get done. Cut hay was taken to the main stackyard where it would rest for six weeks until it all started up again for the second crop. When my relatives helped, they received a portion of the hay for their livestock.

Dad fed his own herd and horses, and any extra hay was sold to other ranchers. Men wearing Stetsons, chaps and boots drove up in big trucks to purchase hay from Dad. They all seemed pleased with these transactions.

Around this time, the saskatoon berries ripened. Out came our picking baskets. Our great-grandmother, Lalma, made baskets for her family, and these were passed on to us. Her fancy ones went for sale. Our baskets had two belt loops so we could wear them around our waists. I loved my basket, which had a design that looked like geese in flight. In the days before grocery stores, our people tied large baskets on their backs to keep both hands free for gathering as much as the family required. Any extra was traded for other goods. Before they began picking the first berry, Mom and Ya-yeh put an offering on the ground to say thanks to the Creator for the gift of such beautiful fruit. Sometimes it was water, sometimes sage, but they never failed to show their gratitude. We witnessed these actions and learned to emulate them. Not to just take and grab the berries from nature, but to stop and remember where they came from. "Never take more than you need" was a familiar reminder. In other words, don't be greedy.

In the berry patch, we were sternly reminded to pick rather than eat. If we saw a yellow dot on a berry, we had to toss it out. This meant that a moth had laid its egg and a worm was growing inside it. Mom made tasty jam and pies with her berries, while Ya-yeh poured her pickings on drying racks for a winter treat. They looked like raisins.

Ya-yeh once rode her horse up to the mountains to pick berries and camp alone for two days. When a black bear came near, she spoke to it in our language and told it to go far away, that there were enough berries for the both of them.

"*Ka wix ha. Chuks ta ma xe'a*", she told the bear. She wasn't afraid. The bear turned and went elsewhere. When she had picked enough berries, she came home. This story reminded me of the Elder's teachings to respect all of nature.

"The land is watching you," they said.

This meant we were never to be careless or wasteful. We must show respect to the land, water and wildlife at all times. "The land remembers…" was a stark reminder to take care.

One time, after picking our quota of saskatoons, Dad saddled up the horses so all of us could ride to the river for a swim. Dad took a rolled-up gunny sack out of his saddle bag. Inside was an iron spear that he had made, which he lashed onto a pole for salmon fishing. It was against the law to fish, but Dad had a craving for fresh salmon. If caught, his gear could be taken, and he would have to pay a fine. He went a distance away from us noisy children and caught a few fish before we headed home. Mom was happy as she cooked them up for supper. As usual, Austin and

I fought over who got to eat the fish eyes; we liked them best. Anytime Dad caught several salmon, he preserved them in a large container of salt. When Mom wanted to cook fresh-tasting fish, she simply rinsed off the salt. It was her favourite meal. We knew Dad also recited his thanks quietly to the Creator for providing the fish for our family and for keeping the warden away that day.

We didn't have electricity, so we used an icebox to keep our food cool. It was always a great mystery to me as to where the big chunks of ice came from in the middle of summer. We later learned that Dad chopped ice in mid-winter to keep frozen in sawdust under the soil in the barn. Food preservation was very important in our home, and we learned not to be wasteful. One of the first prayers Ya-yeh taught us was to thank the Creator for the healthy food that gives us life.

"Say the words, *kwuks chemxw O ła kwuk pi,* which means 'Thank you to the High Chief.'

Always be grateful to the Creator," she told us. *Xwuy mlamxtip he s ła'xans* "Bless the food."

THE SUMMER BEFORE SCHOOL — 1957

In mid-August of 1957, at age six, I rode with my parents in our truck to Kamloops. A tomato farmer needed workers to pick his field, and he offered payment plus boxes of tomatoes to anyone willing to work. Austin stayed home with Ya-yeh.

At the farm, I was told to stay in the vehicle while the adults worked because there were snakes in the field. A girl my age named Odelia joined me, and we quickly became friends. We discussed whether the word "thirsty" was the same as the word "Thursday." We laughed at our confusion and decided to go to school on thirsty and drink water when we're Thursday.

The end of August brought huckleberries. These were the best berries: purple, juicy, sweet and tart. We rode up to the Coquihalla Mountains in our truck and set up a tent. Dad built a campfire, Mom cooked meals, and we picked berries together for hours. This was our summer holiday before school started in September. Us kids played tag, hide-and-seek and kick-the-can for a break. Making noise kept the bears away. Sometimes we woke to fresh snow in the morning. When our fingers felt frozen or our clothes got wet, we warmed ourselves by the fire.

"Fill those baskets you kids. I don't want to see purple mouths," Dad warned us.

Mom wasn't as strict. She called huckleberries *medicine food*. She told us medicine food helped our spirits become strong in times of sadness. She liked being in the same mountains where she picked berries with her grandparents as a little girl. She felt close to them in the hills and shared many good memories with us such as riding on a wagon pulled by horses. She reminisced about all her brothers and sisters together feeling jolly and free, and getting away from the town of Merritt for a spell. It was exciting for her to meet up with cousins to play games after picking. Imagining Mom as a child was difficult because she was the one who nurtured us in everything.

We never went hungry in the mountains. Mom had lots of food cooked and ready to eat. Dad mainly patrolled the area for bears and cougars with his rifle to ensure we were safe. If he shot a deer, that was a bonus. Roasted ribs on the campfire a delicacy.

Life was fun when another child came to our camp. We often got to see cousins and relatives when we were in the mountains. It was like a family reunion before school started. Dad's friend brought his six-year-old daughter named Jessie. They were from the Okanagan tribe and lived near Nicola Lake. Dad understood their language, and they spoke together for hours when they visited. Jessie fit right in with our family. We figured out that we'd both be starting grade one at Kamloops Indian Residential School in September and promised to stay friends. We acted happy and brave, but I felt scared of the big brick school my older siblings attended.

Those of us status Indians were required by law to attend residential schools. My family attended Kamloops Indian Residential School. Many of my relatives didn't have status, so they remained in Merritt to attend public school. I envied them and asked Mom if Dad could give up his status so I wouldn't have to go to Kamloops. We'd lose our land if he did, she said.

When it was time for me to go to school, everyone coached me to "remember your English name, Mary Jane." I repeated it over again, but promptly forgot. The name Mary came from my dad's sister. I was proud to carry her name because she was a good woman, but I just couldn't get used to it. I was taught to say *Injowa Nk'xetko,* which means "I am Nk'xetko." I was confused by the new name Mary Jane. It sounded too elegant for someone like me who climbed trees, stored worms in her pockets and hung around in the blacksmith shop.

KAMLOOPS INDIAN RESIDENTIAL SCHOOL

In the past we said goodbye to my older siblings, then we travelled back to Joeyaska to a quieter house. Suddenly, it was my turn to enter this strange new world. My older sisters went off to their dorms after repeating the rules and regulations I would need to remember to stay safe. It appeared they had forgotten how lost and lonely first school days were.

"Never go here, stay away from there, keep to your dorm, never, ever come to our dorms. It's against the rules. Don't contact us for anything. You'll get into big trouble if you set foot in other dorms looking for us. Listen to all the rules of your supervisor. Obey her and you'll do okay," they told me.

I willed myself to believe them. The sights and smells were foreign to me.

My parents said goodbye and drove away, and my sisters disappeared. Older girls in my dorm introduced me to Sister Thomasa, who served as the junior girls' guardian and supervisor. She sounded strict and stern. My mind went blank, and I couldn't recall my English name, so I ran off in a panic to find my sister, Shirley. If caught, I would have been in trouble, but I didn't care. Shirley told me to repeat "Mary Jane" on all ten fingers until it stuck. I felt reassured, but she instructed me not to come see her again as it was against the rules. I returned to the junior girls' rec room. Sister Thomasa assigned me the number '39,' and that's what she called me from then on.

I was told to put my personal belongings and clothing into my suitcase, which would be stored in a room called the Linen Room. Any money would be locked in there as well. I received new jeans, T-shirts, flannel nightgowns, underwear, socks and a navy tunic for school. Each item had to be marked with my number, 39.

An older girl checked my head for lice, cut my hair very short then doused it with kerosene. Every junior girl received the same haircut. She bathed me, dressed me in my new clothes and sent me out to the playground to wait for the supper bell.

I felt different. I *looked* different. I was lost and alone, my stomach sick with fear. There was a playground, but many of us girls felt strange and out of place so we sat on a bench and stared at the brick wall across the yard. Waiting in silence.

A door opened.

"Sister Charlene," someone whispered.

A tall, skinny nun who taught grade six walked so smoothly in her long black dress that it appeared she didn't have feet and was floating toward us. She carried two wastebaskets full of papers. She pointed to me and called me over to take one of the baskets to the incinerator with her. I obeyed and followed her to a place I thought I had been told was out of bounds for students. She opened the incinerator lids, snatched the basket from me, emptied the contents into the smoldering fire, shut the lids, took her baskets and went on her way without looking at me. I returned to the playground bench.

The supper bell sounded, and we filed indoors to wash our hands and line up in the long, empty hallway. Sister Thomasa called me out in front of everyone.

"Number 39! You were at the incinerator!" she yelled.

"Yes, Sister," I replied.

She pulled a thick leather strap with pointed metal prongs on the end from inside her sleeve. She instructed me to hold out my hands and I obeyed.

"You are not allowed to go near the incinerator!" she yelled, raising the strap high.

I told myself not to cry, but when she brought it down with all her strength onto my outstretched hand, I shrieked in terror and blacked out. I can't recall anything after that—not my teacher, my friends nor my classroom. There are no memories; two years are missing from my life.

AT HOME IN JOEYASKA — SUMMER 1958

Kamloops Indian Residential School students were permitted to go home for summer holidays, and my memory returns in 1959 at Joeyaska for one single instant. Mom was cooking at the wood stove, stirring something in a pot. I stood on a block of wood nearby playing with a grey metal handle that opened a side slot on the stove.

I can barely recall this moment in time. It was as if I crawled slowly and carefully through a dark tunnel into the light. I summoned all my courage and said, "I hate school, and I don't want to go back there."

"No. You have to go back. It's the law," she replied quietly, not looking at me.

I froze, trying to wrap my brain around the fact that we had no choice in the matter. The shock of being forced to return to such a dangerous place caused me to crawl back into that dark tunnel and enter a dark space, deep inside myself where I could feel safe. I have no memories after this for one and a half years.

GRADE TWO AT SCHOOL — 1958

My Grade two year was totally blank. There are no remembrances at all. I have a sense that as a seven year old child in the entirety of my life at home and at school I was shell shocked. I copied what everyone else was doing and followed along.

A picture was taken of me during the summer of 1959. Robert and Austin stand to my right. Shirley squats by Austin. The field is empty which meant it was after haying season. I look at the picture, but have no memories whatsoever.

I want to attach that picture here.

GRADE THREE AT SCHOOL — 1959

My memories resurface in November 1959 when our grade three class was preparing for the Christmas concert. Our teacher, Mrs. Gerta, pitied me and tried to coax me into playing Rudolph. She held up a red ball for my nose and explained that this was the most important role in the song. I couldn't bring myself to participate though, even when she lined up six children behind her and they began prancing around like the reindeer in the song. Mrs. Gerta was annoyed, but she eventually gave up. I kept my head down and went through the motions of being a student in the classroom. Never speaking, not yet ready to emerge.

School routine was very strict and scary for me. The bell clanged every morning to wake us up. We washed our faces at the sinks and dressed in school uniforms. Everyone of us felt the pressure to get ready for the next assignment. We lined up for breakfast of either porridge or cold cereal such as corn flakes, with watered down powder milk. A cup of watery hot cocoa was placed at the tables for each one of us. Ten of us sitting on benches at one table. Sometimes we got a glass of what looked like chalk water, we were forced to drink it. I recall gagging it down. For years I was convinced it was powdered chalk. Later I found out it was powdered milk. I knew what milk was because of Mom's milk cow back home.

When everyone got their meals and was seated, a nun led the meal time prayer, "Bless us O Lord and these thy gifts which we are about to receive from thy bounty. Amen."

After that we could eat. A nun patrolled, reminding us not to talk, but to eat everything, don't throw anything out. When everyone at our table finished her meal, we asked permission to get up and go quietly back to our rec rooms where we did minimal chores and got ready to go to class. If someone forgot to ask permission and got up, the nun made them wait for the whole dining hall to finish their meal before letting that table go. In silence.

In spring or autumn weather, we wore sweaters but in winter we put on boots, coats and hats. Everyday we lined up and went out the doors to our classrooms. If no adult was in the vicinity we talked and laughed, sometimes somebody shouted out in sheer relief because of the tension forced on us so early in the day.

If an adult accompanied us to the school building, we walked in silence.

At ten o'clock every morning a bell rang for recess which meant going outdoors to the Playground. Girls didn't go near the boys, we mainly walked around, or someone instigated tag In which case we chased around, yelled and relaxed a little before the next bell or whistle rang to bring us back into the classrooms to finish up morning lessons.

At noon we lined up to go back to the main building to get ready for lunch, putting coats into lockers, washing hands and lining up to go into the dining hall in silence. Afterward we headed to our classes at one. The bell rang at 3:30 to let us out so we could go back to our rec rooms, get a snack of either an apple or a hard biscuit, then we had free time to go outdoors for some fresh air before supper. Every group had similar but separate schedules.

Life was regulated throughout each day. Friday evening was movie night in the gym.

Saturday was cleaning day for the seniors and intermediate students, less strict for the junior girls, grades one through four. We were required to line up at the chapel to confess our sins every Saturday. In lineup I never knew what to confess. I was too ashamed to ask forgiveness for the secret hatred and bitterness I felt for those who treated us cruelly, so I'd ask a girl nearby, "What do you say to the priest?" I heard, "make up some transgression,"

"I told a lie, or cursed, or I had bad thoughts." The priest would listen politely, I was glad he didn't require the details. He forgave me and told me to go do penance, "Go kneel at the main altar and recite ten Hail Mary's." Then the ordeal was over.

Sunday meant everyone went to mass in the main chapel. We wore special skirts.

Girls wore tams. We sang hymns, knelt, then stood, then sat and listened to the priest pray in Latin. On our best behavior at all times. We all had to go up to the altar for holy communion.

Weekends meant relaxing, I attributed it to our supervisors needing a rest from scolding, yelling and glaring at us. They needed to fill up.

Junior girls had more outdoor time in the playground, or going for walks down the road.

A religious course called catechism was taught in school every day, presented with great seriousness, a reminder about hell and damnation awaiting transgressors. None of it made any sense to me. Especially purgatory and limbo. I went through the motions of listening, following along with the crowd and wishing it would end soon. It appeared to be a message to frighten us into heaven, keep us out of hell by putting us through a form of agony every day.

Walking down any long hallway became a fearsome activity. When hearing footsteps and the rattling of those long rosary beads nuns wore on their skirts meant trouble. One time my friend darted into a broom closet in the corner rather than face a scolding, leaving me alone to face an angry tirade just for walking within any supervisor's eyesight. Supervisors needed to remind us they held the power at all times, day and night. No one dared challenge them. It appeared to be a dictatorship and we knew where we stood.

We lived at the school for two hundred and eighty-eight days every year, but it felt like an eternity.

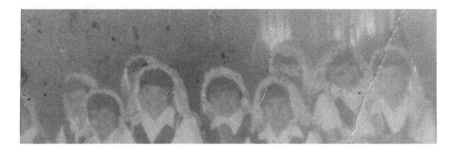

CHRISTMAS HOLIDAYS AT HOME IN JOEYASKA — 1959

My parents took us home after the Christmas concert. The heater in Dad's truck didn't work well, but it didn't matter. It was a sixty-mile ride along frozen Nicola Lake back to Joeyaska, and the farther we rode away from the residential school, the warmer my heart became.

I relaxed and grew accustomed to home-cooked meals and family life again. My sister Deanna had some money, so she took me shopping with her to Armstrong's Department Store in Merritt. We chose peppermint candy canes, gumdrops, Humbugs and walnuts in the shell. I watched her purchase a lovely brush and comb set and pay for all of these items at once.

At home, Dad kept the fire in the wood stove going day and night. We sat at the table putting jigsaw puzzles together and eating our fill of nuts and candies. No one ever felt hungry at home—not like the hunger we felt at school, which was an emptiness that settled in the pit of my stomach. We weren't numbers anymore. We called each other by our names. We became family—siblings, sons and daughters—once again, and we felt complete. My two older brothers popped in for visits and to drop off gifts, but they had jobs and lives elsewhere.

I was happy. No longer silent and downcast, I laughed, sang, and whistled in pure glee until shushed by family members who wanted to hear the news or Christmas carols on the radio. On Christmas Day, everyone opened gifts from under the tree. Deanna handed me a package, saying it was from Santa Claus. I opened it and recognized the brush and comb set from the store. I was disappointed to learn that Santa wasn't real but elated to receive my own comb and brush. At school, borrowing someone else's comb was risky; you could get nits. My happiness was short lived, however. Back at school, someone stole the set from my locker, and I was sad to lose that small remembrance of joyful times spent at home.

During the holidays, Deanna shared some surprising news: Mrs. Gerta wanted to adopt me. She had even asked my parents, but they said no. I felt a rush of excitement that someone wanted me, followed by horror at the thought of being separated from my family. What a relief that her bid for me was ultimately unsuccessful. Mom was my security. When we were away from each other, I felt her warm arms around me. I felt I couldn't live without her. At school, I continually whispered the words, *uhan ha nesux inskixze*: "Where do you go, my mother?" I repeated these words in my mind over and over.

DEPARTMENT OF CITIZENSHIP AND IMMIGRATION				
INDIAN AFFAIRS BRANCH				
SCHOOL SUBJECTS				
—	FALL	WINTER	SPRING	FINAL
Basic Subjects				
HEALTH	B	B	B	A
ORAL READING	B	B	A	A
SILENT READING			A	A
WRITING	B	A	A	A
SPELLING	C+	B	A	A
LITERATURE				
ARITHMETIC	B	B	C+	B
SOCIAL STUDIES	D	C	C	C
SCIENCE	D	C-	C	A
OUR INDIAN SCHOOLS ENCOURAGE EACH PUPIL TO LEARN				
AGRICULTURE				
RELIGIOUS INSTRUCTION	D	B	B	B

Certificate of Promotion

This certifies that *Mary Jane Sterling* has completed satisfactorily the course prescribed for Grade *VI* and was promoted to Grade *VII* on the *17* day of *June* 19*55*

G. P. DUNLOP OMI .....PRINCIPAL

LIFE AT SCHOOL

I was getting accustomed to the school routine and found some of my schoolmates to be friendly, we were all in the same situation. When school was out for the day, we had to change out of uniforms and into jeans then sit down on the floor by our lockers. Two of the strongest girls brought in a box of red delicious apples for our snack. Brother Spencer tended the orchard near the school grounds and threatened anyone who came near. Wild stories of Brother Spencer acting like a monster chasing away children who tried to steal his apples was enough to keep us away from there. Those apples were sweet and juicy, he must have done something right. Each of the dorms got their daily quota of cod liver oil, vitamins and apples.

After snack time we had one hour of play time outdoors before the supper bell rang. Mostly we got into groups to play games such as, "What time is it Mr. Wolf" or "Red Rover Come Over" and the popular "Red Light Green Light." Playing together, yelling, laughing and enjoying freedom without supervisors was a bonus. However, being a small skinny kid, I was usually picked last on any team and generally spent most of my time wishing I could be invisible. When I got picked on or scolded, that's when I wished the floor would open up to swallow me. To be a shy and cautious child at school put a lot of pressure on me. I needed to stay in my safe zone.

I always had one or two friends. We were like pals. We played together, talked of our parents and how much we missed home life. Gave each other pushes on the swings, shared the teeter totters. Whenever we walked anywhere, we walked together hand in hand, happy for a little while. One day our supervisor announced,

"No more holding hands. Not even with your sisters." That came as a shock and we didn't understand why.

Our supervisor, Sister Cleo, was a very impatient nun. I kept my distance from her because she was quick to get angry and yell at us. If we found ourselves walking in front of her, she would curl her fingers into a pointy fist and jab us, exclaiming,

"Get out of my way you amathon!" I looked up "amathon" in an old English dictionary; it meant "idiot." If we made a mistake, she shouted, "You'll never amount to anything! What a dummy. You never learn."

Because of these interactions and others like it, I felt scared most of the time, but never so much as I did in the dorm at night after the lights were shut off. In the junior girls' dorm on the third floor, only one red "exit" light glowed in the middle of the night. Sister told us not to get up to walk around because the devil lived in the dark under our beds. Her threats worked; we were terrified, and I slept in the middle of my cot, afraid to move.

Sometimes I woke to the sound of a girl sniffling and crying nearby. I would carefully peek out to see someone standing as still as a statue. Then I'd hear what sounded like water trickling on to the floor. The girl had wet her pants, too terrified to walk down the hall to the bathroom. Afraid to move, I willed myself to go back to sleep.

Other times I'd hear a shout, "Mommy, help!" Occasionally, those voices also woke up Sister Cleo. Peering from under my blanket, I watched her emerge from her nearby bedroom in a black veil and white nightgown. Sister Cleo would calm down the one yelling, telling her to be quiet and go back to sleep. When everything settled, I would whisper into the darkness *xwist memin kin*: "I want to go home."

I had my own terrifying nightmares in which gigantic monsters chased me. I would run as fast as I could, but I was too small and slow to escape. I'd gasp frantically for breath; that's when I'd faint and blackout in my dreams. It felt like being suffocated. After those nightmares, when dawn was breaking, I'd wake gingerly. My tight fists released, my breathing became easier, and the tension in my body started to fade. Sometimes my bladder relaxed as well, and I felt a warm liquid release, realizing too late that I had wet my bed.

Everyone knew the yelling, shaming and blaming that took place when one had an "accident" in the night. If I could get up early enough, I would run to the bathroom and rinse out my bottom sheet, later secreting it down to the laundry room without Sister knowing. It didn't happen often, but it was devastating when it did. We certainly didn't invite more shame and guilt to be heaped on us. But controlling our tiny bodies' responses to our stressful surroundings was sometimes beyond our reach. Residential school had a way of making you feel like everything bad in the world was your fault.

My friend Lena told me about one time when she woke in the middle of the night being carried out of Sister Thomasa's bedroom. She didn't know why, and she had no idea what had happened.

FOLK DANCING

In grade three, Sister Cleo ordered some of us to become dancers. No one had any choice in the matter. The school had a folk dancing troupe called the Kamloops Indian Residential School Folk Dancers. It was founded in the 1950s and grew to become an amateur group of forty girls who performed songs and dances in different towns for fundraising projects.

One time we performed in a big hall packed with men in cowboy hats. They were the Cattlemen's Association who requested our group as entertainment for their annual meeting. It was a rip-roaring event, and they hooted, whistled and cheered after every song and dance. Occasionally, we travelled to Merritt to perform in the high-school gym. Mom and Dad, sitting amongst my schoolmates' parents, were thrilled for us to be on stage and smiled at us from the front row. I wanted to leap down and go home with them.

We travelled to many other cities, usually by bus. Once, we went by train to Revelstoke. For overnight trips, we were billeted with families who fed us breakfast and packed us bag lunches for the ride back to school. I generally sat on the bus with one of my older sisters.

The nuns taught us a Hungarian kerchief dance, a Polish mazurka, a Mexican hat dance, a French minuet, a Sailor's hornpipe, an array of Irish jigs and reels, along with various songs. My sisters quickly learned the steps to each routine and became lead dancers. They attributed their skill to the music played in our home. Whenever we had visitors, Dad would bring out his fiddle and guitar, sing songs and get us dancing around the living room. The adults liked to waltz to a song called "Magic in the Moonlight," which they sang with gusto. I recall my aunts and uncles smiling and stepping in time to the rhythm.

As a little dancer, I was assigned to a group of four doing an Irish reel. We sidestepped to the left and to the right, linked arms, danced around each other, formed circles, lined up and finished with a bow. If we made a mistake or stepped out of tune during our daily practices, Sister Cleo swatted our feet, ankles and shins with a stick. It was difficult to remember our steps while also trying to evade her blows.

For one particular performance on stage, I was bedecked in a cute costume, bonnet and lipstick. I was keeping time to the music with my dance partners, till I caught Sister Cleo glaring at me backstage. I froze, lost my rhythm and forgot the steps. I have no idea how that routine finished because I blacked out in fear. Sister Cleo was such a stickler for perfection, you can imagine the hollering that followed. My fear of her outweighed my fear of being on stage.

The girls at school who weren't dancers envied us for travelling around the province, seeing new sights. Little did they know that they were the lucky ones, escaping early morning practices, hours of bus travel and endless rehearsals. We were berated for our mistakes and never recognized for a job well done. Our classroom teachers also resented us for missing school. Being a dancer was its own unique form of torture. We dreaded it.

Occasionally we danced in a jail or prison. The inmates were grateful for music, song and dance. After a performance, I sometimes noticed men's faces stained with tears. We were humbled because we also understood what it meant to live life behind walls and according to someone else's strict rules and regulations.

HOME AT EASTER — 1960

The first day home during Easter holidays, Austin and I followed Dad around on his morning chore of mending broken barbwire fences past the gooseberry patch. Fences kept other animals from getting in and kept our livestock from getting out. If our cattle or horses wandered onto public roads, my parents could lose their animals or incur a fine to get them back.

It was wood-tick season, and our parents warned us not to roll on the ground or pickup dead foliage. We quickly forgot those warnings, tossing sticks and dried leaves at each other, ducking under branches and hiding behind trees until it was time to go back home. We raced toward the house. I almost let Austin win, but decided to run faster and burst through the door first. Mom had a tub of soapy water ready. I had to get in for a bath so she could check my hair and clothing for ticks. Sure enough, she found three wood ticks on my neck.

"I warned you about the wood ticks," she scolded Dad as soon as he and Austin walked through the door. "She's got three. Aus probably has a dozen."

"Oh, these kids are so disinfected from Indian school that no bug is going to bite their hides," said Dad.

At Easter, Dad purchased a bucket of vanilla ice cream for dessert. After polishing off the ice cream in our bowls, Austin and I started a tug of war for the bucket, not realizing that the top had a sharp metal rim. The rim sliced the four fingers of my left hand, and I screamed with pain and at the sight of my own blood. Dad, an army veteran, stopped the blood flow, cleaned the wounds and bandaged me up. Mom changed my bandages and made covers that looked like little pockets to fit over my fingers. My wounds healed by the time Easter holidays came to an end and we returned to school, but the scars spoke to the danger that sometimes lurked in seemingly innocent things.

SPRING AT SCHOOL

Back at school, we returned to our regular routines: bells, uniforms, line-ups and baths on Wednesdays and Saturdays. Because of my hazel eyes and fair skin, I was picked on by older girls who seemed to resent me. Four hundred students attended our school, and only a few of us looked different from everyone else. This singled me out in the eyes of the nuns and my schoolmates. Someone glaring at you with a nod was a threat that meant "I'm going to get you." I felt alone and helpless.

Sister Cleo told us to pray to God about anything that caused us worry. Before bed, I would get on my knees and desperately ask God to change my eyes to brown. In the morning, I would run to the mirror, anticipating a transformation. Eventually I gave up in disappointment. I had no one to confide in and no one to protect me, so I kept my head down and avoided eye contact. Within our family unit we were cherished no matter what colour eyes we had. When I complained to Mom, who had dark brown eyes, she told me that the Creator knows what is right for us.

During this particular spring, my older brother Fred, a fine athlete trained with the province's Golden Gloves boxing club. Father Francis arranged for him to come to our school to put on an exhibition match against a German boxer. Students filled the bleachers in the gym to witness the bout. Prior to the match, he came to get me from the junior girls' rec room. He held my hand as we walked together down the hall toward the gym, and the other girls looked on with surprise and envy.

"Holy, is that your big brother?" they asked.

I just smiled. After that, when bullies picked on me, I looked them in the eye and told them that my brother Fred would deal with them. Bullying from schoolmates stopped, and I could breathe easier. Unfortunately, this approach didn't work with the nuns.

AT HOME WITH MY BROTHER
AUSTIN — SUMMER 1960

Austin and I were following Dad through the field to the haystack one Sunday morning. We got distracted midway and fell into a disagreement about something. We wrestled on the ground and were soon covered in dirt, grass and dried straw. We saw a big sedan drive up to Dad, then it stopped beside us. It was Father Francis from the residential school in Kamloops. He was headed to the Coldwater reserve to say mass in the church. Dad had given his blessing for Father Francis to invite us along. We pulled ourselves up, shook ourselves off and climbed into the back seat of his big car. We forgot what we had been fighting about. We were happy to go somewhere to do something different and were suddenly on our best behaviour.

The little church in Coldwater was built on land given by my great grandfather, Ya-yeh's father, when he was a chief in the 1800s. I liked that church. My family attended many functions there, and many of our ancestors were buried in the cemetery nearby. Austin and I were the only ones in attendance that day. Usually there'd be a few people who came out, but they must have been away doing chores or running errands. We sat in the front pew quietly. I turned to look at Austin and gasped. His shirt was on backwards and inside out, and there was dried straw in his uncombed hair. We both looked unkempt, wearing old clothes that we'd probably slept in. We'd heard that people went to hell for less serious offences.

At residential school, we wore clean, pressed clothing to church. Every hair was in place. Perhaps God wouldn't accept us unless we were spotless on the outside as well as on the inside? I was speechless that Father Francis didn't mind our current state. Didn't he recall our whole student body attending mass at school dressed in our Sunday best? While Austin and I waited, I picked the hay and straw from his hair and clothing. I asked him to clean me up too, hoping we wouldn't get into another fight right there in church. We often fought over anything or nothing. Others said we were like bear cubs wrestling around all the time. Father didn't appear to notice our unkempt appearance and went through the steps of Sunday mass. When it was over, he thanked us politely for attending. He gave us his special sprinkle of holy water and formally shook our hands before returning us home.

Austin and I were on our best behaviour after that blessing. My parents invited Father Francis to stay for supper, and he enjoyed chatting with Dad. Mom was a great cook and prepared fresh vegetables from the garden. I admired our dinner table with its fine, colourful vegetables and fried deer steak cooked to perfection. Dad never set foot in a church, nor attended mass. I was convinced he wouldn't make it to heaven when he died, but he didn't seem worried. We saw him praying in the direction of the rising sun certain mornings, speaking words in his language when he didn't know we were listening. He always ended by saying "Hoh."

We rode horses every chance we got. Sometimes visitors who came to see Dad rode up to the house on horseback. They'd dismount and tie their horse to a nearby post before wandering off to talk to Dad. Those horses generally were good riding horses. They were well trained, equipped with saddles and gear, and obedient to a rider—unlike Dad's horse, JW Baldy, who didn't like us kids riding him. He kicked at us, attempted to bite us and shook his head so we couldn't put the bridle on. Cantankerous was the best word to describe him. But when Dad took charge, there was no fooling around on JW's part. He was most co-operative during deer hunts, cattle drives and roundups for branding calves in the spring. Dad was a successful hunter and always came home with a gutted deer in a gunny sack strapped to the back of his saddle. He'd tell us how JW would spot the deer first and come to a complete stop, then stare in the direction of the animal in silence, giving Dad a chance to shoot it.

"I wouldn't get a deer if it weren't for JW," he asserted.

The rest of us who'd experienced JW's antics wondered if he was talking about the same horse. I recalled how Shirley enjoyed taking JW for a gallop across the fields. One day I happened to see them when JW got stubborn and came to a sudden stop. Shirley went flying over JW's head, landed on the ground in a sitting position in front of JW, her face beet red. I wasn't concerned because she got up. JW waited and even looked sheepish. She climbed back on and off they went trotting down the road.

One day a man named Willey rode up to visit Dad. He wore a white cowboy hat and silver spurs. His horse, Jock, was decked out in an ornate saddle and reins. It was a sight to see because Dad's tack was no-frills. I asked Willey if I could take his horse for a ride.

"Sure, Jock's a good horse. Go ahead," Willey said, grinning.

He heaved me up on the saddle, and I headed up past the barn toward Godie Canyon. Austin caught sight of me and called, "Hey, I want to go too!" I rode slow while he ran to the corral to get JW. With only a rope around JW's neck and a saddle blanket tied on with another rope, Austin climbed up on a side fence, hopped on and fell into step behind Jock.

Jock was obedient. He moved in any direction I wanted him to. It was too easy. I was accustomed to a stubborn horse that stopped when I wanted to go and turned left when I wanted to turn right. On Jock, I felt in charge. JW was behaving too; that is, until both horses decided they wanted to turn around twenty minutes later. A noise among the quiet pine trees must have spooked them. Ears twitching, eyes alert, they both stepped lively sensing an unseen danger, then turned toward home and raced full out. There was no stopping them. My feet didn't reach the stirrups, so I held on tight. Austin held onto the rope around JW's neck and pulled ahead of Jock in the last few seconds, the saddle blanket twisting round under JW's belly. He won the race and lost the blanket. We made it back to the corral out of breath, but otherwise intact.

We figured the horses schemed to outrun each other. JW needed to win every race. Austin and I didn't say much, glad to be alive but especially glad that no adult saw. We would have been scolded for being too wild on those horses. I returned Jock to the fence by the house and slid down off the saddle. Willey was smiling, ready and waiting to go.

"Austin, go open the gate for me" he said, hopping on Jock. "I'll give you a quarter."

We both raced up to the main road to open the gate for Willey and Jock, arriving at the same time. Willey gave us each a quarter, grateful that he didn't have to dismount. We closed the gate behind him, speculating on Willey's wealth. That Jock must have cost a lot of money.

As horse and rider disappeared down the road, the white hat gone from our sight, we discussed how to spend our quarters. We settled on one popsicle and one chocolate bar each. JW innocently munched hay in the corral, saddle blanket draped neatly on the fence.

Later that summer when the hay was put up, our horses were free in the fields. I had nothing to do so I started walking over to my aunt's house toward the field near the highway. A strange horse must have got onto our property, I didn't recognize it. That horse galloped toward me at a furious pace. I stood still not knowing what to do. Suddenly JW Baldy came running faster, whinnying loud. He forced that horse away from me with moments to spare. I looked around to see if anyone witnessed the event. There was no one. I felt shook up and returned to our house wondering if anyone would believe me. At least I'd tell Dad a strange horse got in somehow. He'd deal with it. I gained a new respect for JW who seemed to know enough to protect me in that moment of danger.

SUMMER AT SCHOOL — 1960

It was unusual for us to spend time at the residential school during the summer, but Father Parant, the school principal, arranged for our dance troupe to perform at the Pacific National Exhibition (PNE) when it opened in mid-August in Vancouver. To rehearse our routines, we lived at school for two additional weeks. My sisters quit their summer jobs, and we travelled back to the school to prepare. The weather was hot, and we sweated through each session despite working out in the cooler mornings. Practicing each dance over and over again, day after day, to the same music grew tedious and tiresome, but dips in the swimming pool offered some respite. Outside of practice, those two weeks were casual and relaxed; a stark contrast to the strict school year I was accustomed to.

During free time, we went for walks down the road. Sometimes we went into Kamloops to go window shopping, though we couldn't afford to buy much. Once, a group of five of us walked along the road below Mount Saint Peter and spotted a cement box with a thick metal pipe poking out. It was a remnant of the old reservoir. Water from the mountain used to flow through, but it had dried up. My friends double dared me to walk out on the pipe, which jutted out about twelve feet in the air. I had good balance, so I took the dare. It was easy walking out until I made the mistake of looking down. It was a long, scary walk backwards, balancing my body to match my feet. The girls shouted encouragement with every step, now seriously afraid that I'd fall fifteen feet to the soft sand below. When I made it back safely, I determined to never again accept a double dare. The fear and adrenaline from that near miss lingered in my body for days.

It was time to leave for Mission Indian Residential School where we would stay overnight. In the morning we went for a walk among the lush green shrubs and saw the remains of the old St. Mary's school, foundation and broken bricks on the ground. My sisters and I held a quiet moment remembering Dad had lived here six decades earlier. We couldn't imagine how stark his life had been without family visits for seven years. Then the day of our performance at the PNE meant a scurry of activity. Our music lined up in order of the dance routines on the tape machine had to be double checked, as well as several huge flat boxes packed for our outfits, costumes, headwear and dance shoes. A Greyhound bus arrived, and everything was loaded underneath alongside our suitcases. We settled into our seats. A few girls always sat together at the back of the bus, and I wondered why, so I snuck close to listen and overheard them talking about boys. My sisters bought me things to read on the trip, and we traded comic books with one another. The bus made a few stops along the route for us to buy snacks or use the washroom. The highway along the Fraser River was beautiful. I made sure to stay awake to take in the colourful rock canyons and powerful water surging below.

We performed in an amphitheater with a stage that overlooked the audience who sat side by side in neat rows. Someone guessed that there were two hundred people watching us that day. PNE staff gave us a small room for costume changes in between songs; in the cramped quarters, we bumped into one another, stepping on each other's toes. I was nervous as usual, but our practicing paid off and we got through our performance without errors. There was a sense of relief within the group when it was all over; we could go back to relaxing at home for the remainder of the summer. There was no other benefit to us for performing except a free trip to the PNE to see the sights and try the roller coaster. That didn't compare to swimming at the Coldwater River, eating our fill of deer steaks, dried salmon, saskatoon berries and—best of all—picking huckleberries at our best camp in the mountains.

GRADE FOUR AT SCHOOL — 1960

I was in the dormitory on the fourth floor, my bed under a gabled window. One night I woke up to see a round glowing circular moonlike structure. It had four antennas and was floating in the dark sky. Because of the silence, I felt scared. I went back to sleep. Walking to class the next morning I described the apparition to Father Keeley. He told me it was a "sputnik" that the Russians sent into space. Such a strange, wonderful sight to witness.

Our teacher that fall was Miss Shanada, who was beautiful and strict. She came from an Ojibwe nation in Ontario, and that's about all we knew about her. I was curious about her language and customs, but I decided she wasn't allowed to divulge that. In addition to the regular curriculum of math, science and writing, she taught us interesting facts about Canada and Europe—but nothing about our tribal histories. It appeared our nations didn't exist in Canada's history books. No one talked about it.

Whenever we walked down the street in Merritt, white townsfolk whispered to one another "There go the dirty Indians." I guess that's why Mom dressed us up in clean clothes anytime we had to go to town. We'd comb our hair neat and tidy, always looking our best. I never took offense at being called Indian. At school, the nuns also called us a bunch of dirty Indians.

I always knew that I was Ntle'kepmx because I'd heard my parents say that. They spoke in that language all the time. As a result, I struggled with the English language at school. When the teacher gave directions, I got mixed up and often had to ask someone what the teacher had said. I was confused a lot of the time and never felt intelligent.

I worked especially hard at reading, writing and spelling. During one spelling contest, our class of thirty students lined up against the wall, and the teacher gave us words to spell out loud. If we spelled a word incorrectly, we had to sit down. I made it to the finals in class and only two of us remained. I stumbled on the word *cellar*, spelling it *celler,* the way it sounded to my ear. The other student, a boy from Lillooet, won. The English language was full of mysterious twists. I was determined to read more books and gain more knowledge so I'd stand a chance at winning the next spelling bee.

I was growing accustomed to the school routine and no longer cried myself to sleep every night, as I had in grade three. I blamed Mom and Ya-yeh for doting on me and making me soft. They made me feel so special that the mistreatment I endured at school came as a severe shock. I scolded Mom, asking her why she had to love me so much.

"It wasn't me. It was Ya-yeh," she said.

On Friday evenings, the whole student body lined up outside of their rec rooms and walked over to the gym to watch the latest western, romance or war film. Movie night was the highlight of our week. Many kids saved their boiled egg from breakfast to eat during the show. Those of us who had a few cents purchased penny candies.

During movie night, we had to stay in our groups. and we weren't permitted to sit with our siblings. If I saw my sisters, I could only wave and smile. Nuns and staff were always patrolling to ensure that no fraternizing happened, but I knew some sisters sat together when the lights were turned off. I heard them whispering, their hands intertwined as they cried together quietly, their tears evident when the lights flicked back on. It appeared more convenient for the staff to keep us siblings apart in order to quickly herd us back to our separate dorms. Nor did they seem to want us to be influenced in any way by our families.

One evening, Shirley walked past me in the supper line-up.

"Read the book *Lorna Doone.* You'll enjoy it," she whispered in my ear before running off.

During library hours, I found that book and quickly read it from cover to cover. I admired Lorna's bravery and felt included in the adventure.

Reading provided escape and became my favourite pastime at school. After that I read every book that sounded interesting. The school had a small library with books on shelves from floor to ceiling. I liked to read who the donors were, adults lovingly inscribing children's or grandchildren's names. They were strangers who became just a little more familiar to me. We never had books around at home. Papers were used to light fires in the wood stove.

One film we watched on movie night showed a man getting drunk and acting violent. He went on to try drugs, which was even more worrisome. It brought to mind when Dad got a hold of some alcohol back home. He and his friends started out joyfully, singing songs and telling stories, but this later turned into angry fights. It was illegal for status Indians to purchase alcohol or drink liquor in taverns and pubs, but somehow alcohol showed up. It caused fear amongst us children. One time in the middle of the night, Mom quickly ushered us kids out to the stackyard, a safe place in the summer. Those friends and relatives who were drinking together earlier quickly became enemies. Fights broke out. The next morning, all was peaceful again.

I knelt in private one day and asked God the Creator, *Oɬa Kwuk pi*, the High Chief, to keep me safe from alcohol and drugs. I never wanted to get involved with those things. That prayer stayed with me throughout my life. That was highly important to me.

Ya-yeh, like many Elders, believed in the Creator rather than a Christian God. She taught me to pray. She told me to hold out my hands and keep them clean because, one day, I would stand in front of the Creator with hands outstretched. "Everything I have ever done is written on my hands" became my daily touchstone. The expression *kin taya inaya ak si es kex schu ex*: means "help me today."

"Ask the Creator for help so that all will go well with you," she advised.

At school, we also observed different holidays. Hallowe'en was particularly scary and perplexing. Sister Cleo, our rec room supervisor, loved to put on a hairy gorilla mask, carry a broom, dim the lights and chase us. We were terrified to see a gorilla face on someone wearing a long black dress, so we shrieked and scattered in sheer panic, searching for cover. We hid under the table, but Sister Cleo clubbed at us, catching me painfully with the broom. Other girls opened their lockers and climbed inside.

In my mind I knew it was Sister Cleo, but I froze in fear of the indiscriminate nature of her whacks. She didn't care who she hit. One girl wet her pants from being chased and clubbed. Hallowe'en only lasted for one day each year, but it was memorable for the sheer terror Sister conjured in us. Although it was supposedly fun and games, many of us had welts and bruises on our bodies afterward.

A scary memory that stands out was at the Kamloops hospital when I got my tonsils removed. I laid on the operating table after receiving ether, a sheet covering my lower body. My chest felt cold, and I shivered in fear, so I pulled the sheet up to my neck. Dr. Miley, who stood nearby said, "Give this girl more Ether." I woke that night with a parched throat and was given a glass of cool apple juice. It was a relief to get back to familiar surroundings at the dorm.

Saturday evenings we could relax after baths and before bedtime. Our supervisors the nuns took the evening off and young women from nearby reserves supervised us. I recall one of them liked the song, "In the Mood". She'd play it over and over getting us to dance in time to the beat. Everyone joined in laughing and smiling, stepping together. Other times we all had to sit around the rec room to listen to a schoolmate read a poem or sing a song. "I Found A Peanut" was a popular performance. We were all quite shy. It took courage to stand up in front of an audience, even in front of girls our own ages.

MOM'S SEWING MACHINE

By age ten, I was becoming clothes conscious. Pleated wool skirts were in fashion, and I wrote to my brother Fred asking him to buy me one. I didn't ask Mom because I knew she didn't have money, but Fred was working and making a wage. I even drew a picture of the type of skirt I wanted. He didn't buy one for me but instead sent me a little note with a dollar bill inside. I was ecstatic. That money went into the locked cupboard in the Linen Room where it would be safe until Friday when I could buy candy. It wasn't as good as a pleated skirt, but it came close.

Mom took in sewing for people. She took apart three men's white sailor uniforms and altered them for three skinny teenage girls in our troupe who danced to "The Sailor's Hornpipe." She did a spectacular job, and I was proud of her. I asked if Sister Cleo paid her; she answered no. I asked if Sister Leo thanked her; she answered no.

Mom was kind to us in little ways. When we got home, she warmed up flannel sheets so that we would feel cozy at night. She must have remembered the smooth icy sheets at school.

When we were at home for Christmas that year, Mom gave me a carefully-wrapped present. It was a blue plaid pleated skirt that she had cleverly re-fashioned from something else. The sewing was so neat and tidy that it looked store bought. The pleats were all hand basted so as not to lose their shape. It was carefully ironed and fit me perfectly. I wanted to wear the skirt right away, but she told me to wait until school was back in session. That year, I happily returned to school wearing my new skirt with a white blouse and a blue sweater.

BOY TROUBLE AT SCHOOL

Toward the end of winter, a boy named Steve handed me a folded note in class just before the end of the school day. I knew he liked me because he was always looking at me, but I just snapped my eyes at him and turned away; I wasn't interested. Besides, boys could get you into trouble even for the smallest things. Miss Shanada saw what happened and ordered me to stay after class and give her the note. I put my winter boots and coat on like everyone else and sat waiting at my desk while the other students filed out. A few classmates cast me sympathetic glances. I wondered why Steve didn't have to stay.

While waiting quietly, I noticed a piece of blank paper that looked exactly like the note. I carefully ripped Steve's note to shreds, dropping the pieces into my boot, and folded the piece of paper in a similar fashion. The teacher finally arrived to yank the note from my hand. When she opened it and discovered it was blank inside, she dismissed me with an annoyed "Get out of here."

Back at my rec room, I pieced together the torn note from my boot. It read: "Meet me by the swings at recess. Signed, Steve." I was furious. It was a risky move for such a silly message. As punishment, I didn't speak to Steve or look his way for the rest of the year. I was beginning to notice boys and I liked some of them, but not to the extent of getting scolded for it. Sister Cleo warned us against becoming "Boy Crazy." She told us boys are dirty. In my mind I thought, my brothers are boys, they're not dirty. "Don't ever get into a car with boys," she warned, they can't be trusted. None of us knew what that meant, she didn't explain.

GRADE FIVE AT SCHOOL — 1961

In grade five, I was ten years old. Our teacher, Sister Claudia, assigned us to write about our goals when we finished school. Some girls wanted to be nurses, a few wanted to be movie stars, and one wanted to be a mother. Most boys wanted to go into logging or mechanics, and a few hoped to get rich in ranching. I wrote that I wanted to be a teacher.

The encyclopedia provided helpful information about the teaching profession, but the meaning of the word *curriculum* evaded me. I worked up my courage to ask Sister Claudia what it meant. I expected a scolding, but instead she was pleased with my interest. She looked me in the eye and, with a smile on her face, said, "I think you'll get there." What I didn't include in that assignment was the fact that, from the time I was a little girl, Dad would point me out to his visitors saying, "That's the little teacher." I'd exchange grins with them.

Becoming a teacher must have been important in our family. My brother Robert after high school graduation attended UBC to take teacher training in 1956.

MEMORIES OF MY DAD

Dad had completed grade seven at St. Mary's Indian Residential School in Mission, BC, he could read, write and speak in English. Dad's grandmother Martha was from the Lytton area, and he maintained the Ntle'kepmx language with some of his relatives and schoolmates. He ran away from St. Mary's at the age of fourteen to escape its brutality. Even without deep formal education, members of our community respected Dad's intelligence and wisdom. Visitors came to talk to my dad about land issues and legal rights. Mom served them lunch, and they spent hours talking in serious tones in our language. Many Elders came up to our house on a wagon pulled by a team of horses. When they finished meeting with Dad, they got back on their wagons and returned home. We heard about some of the people who lost their land in exchange for a bottle of whiskey. We heard about the trickery. Dad also interpreted for the police when someone in jail couldn't speak English. He helped them as much as possible to understand the law and their circumstances. One policeman was so grateful he gave Dad a German shepherd pup. Dad named it "Spud."

Dad was an army veteran who'd served as a sniper in World War I. He fought at Vimy Ridge and was wounded at Ypres. Upon recovering in 1919, he arrived home to Joeyaska. I saw photos of him in his uniform with his medals of bravery. He sometimes talked about how well trained the horses were on the battlefield; they held steady despite the loud guns and explosions going off all around them. His Uncle Barnes was so proud of him for serving that he gave Dad his fields at Joeyaska. Barnes died in the 1918 Spanish flu pandemic.

The commanders in the war gave the soldiers rum for courage before each battle. I began to understand how that affected Dad's life during the war and afterwards. He barely survived the chemical agent, mustard gas, and he had a hard time accepting the fact that some of the enemy he shot at were young lads. It bothered him. I once heard him yelling at us like we were the enemy. He had been drinking alcohol with friends, then he switched into soldier mode after they had gone.

"You're at home. We are your family," yelled Shirley in her loudest voice. "There's no enemy here!"

That settled him down, and he came to himself, but the encounter reinforced my desire to steer clear of alcohol. The next morning, he was back to his chores and whistling a tune.

Just one time I recall Mom got drunk. She and Dad yelled at each other. I felt frustrated and ashamed of them, so I yelled out in my loudest voice, "I hate you!" They stopped arguing for ten seconds, looked at me and resumed their fight. The next day was Christmas Day, and Mom didn't cook the special meal. When I woke up in the morning, the stove hadn't been lit, it was cold in the house. My parents were passed out.

Robert and his girlfriend came by with gifts and hoped to enjoy dinner with us. They quickly got the stove going and cooked the turkey, but it wasn't the same without the whole family present. They took off to visit other relatives. When Dad woke, he looked at me and said, "You hate me." I didn't know how to tell him how much I disliked what alcohol did to him, so I asked him if he spoke French over in Europe. He relaxed and said,

"Toute d'suite, oui, oui, m'sieur," we all laughed. Shirley, who stood close by, whispered to me, "Gee, you can be brave sometimes."

Later when Mom joined us, I didn't say a word about how disappointed and betrayed I felt to see her in a drunken state. I thought it was the end of my world. I asked her,

"Why did you do it."

"Everyone urged me to drink more, and I wanted to see what the big deal was. I didn't like it," she said.

One pressure on Dad was the fact that his grandfather Joeyaska held title to his land, when an Indian Agent (without consultation) in 1938 amalgamated our ranch with the Lower Nicola Indian Band located eleven miles beyond the town of Merritt. No Agent or elected Chief assisted Dad to get that rectified after 1955. That's when the highway and the Trans Mountain Pipeline went through our fields with no compensation to the rightful owners. Chiefs promised to help, but once elected they forgot us. My parents felt the threat of losing their land. I saw the anguish it caused Mom and Dad. I felt their helplessness.

Christmas that year slowly got back to regular family time after that; lots of quiet time.

In 1961, Dad dressed up in his only suit and tie for election day. He finally had the right to vote, and he faced the day with a certain reverence. After casting his vote, he and several men stood talking together enthusiastically on the street, seemingly pleased to play a part in politics. I later learned that status Indians had just gained the right to vote. I found it strange that Dad willingly risked his life to fight for Canada in a world war when he didn't even have the right to vote in his own country. No one helped him with his land ownership, yet he was a decorated war veteran. Something didn't add up.

Shortly afterward Status Indians got the right to purchase liquor and drink beer in pubs and taverns. That became a new problem for many families. When Dad finished his work sometimes, he went into the pub to drink beer with friends. If we tagged along, we had to wait in the truck for a long time before he came out. Sometimes he gave us each two dimes which bought a bottle of pop and a bag of cheezies, or, we'd save up our coins for a comic about "Archie and Friends." Going to town after that had lost its appeal.

I saw a photo of Mom and Dad standing in front of our cedar shake house. Deanna explained that Dad purchased the old teacherage at an auction, the house where school teachers lived in the town of Merritt. It took Dad a whole day in 1935 and six teams of horses to move the house up to his land. He had just married Mom, and they needed a home. My mind was speechless at how that was accomplished. One team of horses was a handful. I was learning to gain a new respect for Dad despite his occasional bouts with alcohol.

One time Shirley and I accompanied him to town, which was a treat in itself. On the way home he stopped and parked the truck to clear debris from one of the main ditches that watered the field. He said not to touch the ignition key. But I felt in a silly mood and started playing catch with the key. It landed inside the inner wall between the window and the door. We couldn't get it out. Dad found a stick and gave us kids a spank and sent us home,

"Next time I tell you to do something, you listen." We walked the rest of the way home in disbelief, and with a renewed attitude to obey him in future. I'd heard he removed the inner door with a screwdriver to find the key. He replaced it with no trouble. That was the one and only time he disciplined us. I was surprised and relieved he didn't remind me about it for days like the nuns would have.

SUMMER — 1961

After my older sister Sarah completed grade eleven in 1959, she eloped with a tall, handsome cowboy she'd met on Dad's haying crew the summer before. The following year they had a bonny baby boy. I'd heard she ran off because Dad wouldn't have allowed her and the cowboy to be together otherwise. He was strict like that. At different points that summer, I spent time with my new nephew and enjoyed looking after him. He was the first baby in our midst, and he brought a lot of joy to everyone. Ya-yeh couldn't pronounce his name, Gregory, so she called him Ker-kwa. Our people believed babies are a gift from the Creator.

In August 1961, Sarah decided to accompany her husband to a cabin in the mountains where he had a contract to build fences for a rancher. She invited me along to look after the baby for one week. I kept an eye on him, changed his diapers, prepared his food and formula, and cleaned out baby bottles while his parents worked. It was very quiet there; the only sounds were the rustling of aspen leaves in the wind and a little stream rippling nearby. I tried to keep the boy quiet because I'd heard from Elders that if a baby cried in the woods, a bear would come to investigate since their cubs' cries sounded like those of human babies. Sarah promised to pay me two dollars for one week, and I took my responsibility seriously. I felt grown up.

I kept busy packing water, building fires in the wood stove, heating water, washing dishes, sweeping the floor, hanging bedding outdoors on the fence and getting things ready for the evening meal. I couldn't cook, but I did whatever else needed doing in our small, temporary home. When he woke up, I took him for walks outside and let him crawl on a blanket.

He had a quirky habit of putting his hand up in the air while sound asleep. No matter how snugly I tucked him into the blanket, out came his arm. After a while I gave up. I was glad when Sarah returned home so she could take over and I could relax. It only lasted seven days, after which they brought me back home and paid me. Helping out made me feel important. I learned to love that baby and felt a little less childish myself.

My sister Deanna was going into grade eleven, and she had a summer job at a ranch near the town of Princeton cooking for the crew. On her days off, she came home and spent time with us. She loved the poetry of John Keats and Lord Byron. Sitting at the kitchen table after a meal, she read me page after page. A captive audience for what seemed hours, I squirmed in my chair.

"Thou was not born for death, immortal Bird!" she recited. "No hungry generations tread thee down..."

Ode to a Nightingale didn't impress me at all, and I was desperate to escape.

The next day she made up for it and took me to town to do some shopping. She was very pretty and, as we walked downtown, a handsome cowboy in a red convertible slowly drove by us to whistle at her. *Wow*, I thought, *only the prettiest girls get whistled at*. She put her nose up in the air and ignored him.

"Don't pay any attention to him," she whispered. "Those cowboys are big flirts."

The nuns told us to stay away from strangers: they could never be trusted.

"Don't get lured in by men you don't know," was a familiar warning from Sister Cleo as she pointed her finger at us and stared into our eyes.

It was against the rules to socialize with boys at school. We were lucky if we could talk to them for more than thirty seconds. It mystified me as to how we could ever get to know them. At home Dad was strict too.

GRADE SIX AT SCHOOL — 1962

It appeared to be against the law to talk about heritage or traditions. No one spoke about it, but we noticed it. That persisted since the 1920's when Mom attended school, a strict rule which separated us from any and all family, cultural influences. Miss Purdeau, a tall, striking Cree woman from James Bay in Ontario, taught our grade six class. Like other Indigenous teachers, she didn't disclose anything about her nation or background. She wore stylish slim-cut dresses, high-heeled shoes and dark red lipstick. Her black hair was cut short in a page boy style, and she wore shiny gold eyeglasses. All of us girls wanted to be just like her when we grew up. Confident and smart, she walked with purpose. Every click of her heels smacked of business.

My grades began to improve in grade six, and I liked seeing the higher marks. However, this inspired snide comments from other students.

"Miss Know It All. Think you're smart, hey?" they quipped. I didn't let on that my older siblings encouraged me to get good grades. That was important. I wanted my family's approval. I would rise to their level, not lower myself.

Teachers gave students with good grades special tasks. Miss Purdeau assigned my friend and I to water her plants in the classroom before the bell rang at one o'clock. After being teased unmercifully by a few of the boys one day, I hatched a plan to put a dab of glue on the desks where they sat. In my mind, their pants would get stuck and they would stop teasing us. But when class started, the boys complained of glue on their pants and Miss Purdeau demanded to know who did it. I owned up. She whacked my hands with a ruler, and it hurt so much I almost cried. I had learned my lesson, but that wasn't the end of it. Someone must have reported me.

Sister Cleo called me forward after school and shouted at me for the stupid prank. In front of everyone she reminded me of my stupidity for days. Crying, I ran to find Shirley in the senior dorm. I wanted her to comfort and reassure me that I would survive this. That was the wrong thing to do. Shirley grabbed my hand and confronted Sister Cleo.

"Why do you keep yelling at my sister every day?" she demanded.

Sister countered that we were in big trouble now; the school principal would punish us. As we both cried, Shirley whispered in my ear, "Let's tell Dad about this." Sister must have heard that because the scolding stopped there. My teachers never brought up the glue incident, and the boys whose teasing prompted my retribution didn't speak to me for the rest of the school year. Those Kamloops Indian Reserve boys liked to tease us girls.

Sarah had a medical appointment in Kamloops one day, and she brought her son to the school for a quick visit. I loved to see family and receive a bag of candy. Sister Cleo walked by and said hello to Sarah. My nephew stared up in shock at Sister who was dressed from head to toe in black and asked, "Are you a witch?" We were speechless, but Sister just laughed and went on her way.

I was still in the school dance troupe, but the long hours of practice, never-ending new steps and routines and teachers' orders—"Point your toes!" "Lift your knees higher!" "Smile!"—were wearing on me. One day, when I was feeling particularly humiliated and sore from the corrective swats, I confided in a girl from Merritt who I thought could be trusted. I told her I was going to quit the dance troupe; I hated it and I'd had enough. She shared this with Sister Cleo behind my back and, when everyone assembled for the supper lineup, I was called forward and yelled at once again.

"You think you can quit the dance troupe, do you?" Sister shouted. "Well, who do you think you are? For punishment, you will polish all the dancing shoes."

I had to clean, polish, and shine forty pairs of black shoes. It was a dirty chore, but I did it. My confidant's betrayal was worse than anything Sister could dole out. Shirley came by and whispered in my ear, "Don't worry, we all have to go through this at one time or another."

SUMMER AT HOME — 1963

Ya-yeh showed me a photo of her father that was taken in 1894. He was the chief back then. I asked Mom if that meant he was high and mighty. But her answer surprised me.

"Chiefs are chosen because they are good hunters, good leaders. They look after the people and make sure everyone is cared for. If not, they get strung up on a tree by their ankles for a short time to learn a lesson." It sounded like a huge responsibility.

The first residential schools opened in the late 1880's. Ya-yeh had a chance to attend, but her mother Qwas'lametko said no because she'd already heard bad things about those schools. Besides, she didn't want her only daughter to lose her language and traditions and grow up to be 'useless'.

Dad knew all the local ranchers in the valley. When his own hay was put up sometimes, he took on haying contracts to put up other folk's hay in the summer. I recall living in a tent for a few days at Whiteford's Ranch near Nicola Lake. After Dad mowed the fields, and the hay dried, a crew assembled to pile, stook and load it into the stackyard. Mom was the cook for those men who worked up big appetites and enjoyed a tasty meal. We had to wait till they finished at our makeshift table, then we could eat. It felt like an adventure, among rolling hills and clear rippling waters, we spent the time looking for little fish, frogs and toads in the creek.

Austin and I were invited up to a ranch one weekend at Nicola Lake by his friend Cal. We could help with chores and kitchen duties. Cal's mom liked having a girl around the place for a change. It was a little holiday for us. Cal spoke a few words in our language so I asked him what my name Nk'xetko meant. He said, "ko means water, I think your name means

"Water Lily." I felt so pleased that I had a name that described a flower. I felt special.

On our last day, his dad saddled up three horses for us to ride around the fields and trails. At the end of the long ride, Cal challenged us to a race for home. The horses obliged and galloped hard. I was in the lead as we neared the house, but Cal's mom must have lowered the clothesline and my horse headed straight for it. I ducked down, leaning over in the saddle to avoid getting knocked off. Luckily, no one got hurt and no adults witnessed what could have been a bad fall. I was thankful to ornery JW Baldy for teaching me so many different strategies. From the way the boys snickered, I suspected they had orchestrated the near miss as a joke. If this is what it meant to be treated like one of the guys, I would take a pass.

Upon returning home I checked with Mom asking if my name indeed meant Water Lily. No, she broke it down and translated it.

"Nk means to cut with a sharp knife, xet means to pierce the deer bone, ko means water. A name that meant I was to become a good cook."

I was disappointed, but I liked the idea of cooking the bone marrow, a delicious healthy treat. Whenever our family sat at the table eating bread covered with hot bone marrow, there was no talking. We were lost in a world that seemed to connect us with the land, with our ancestral traditions and the healthy food that sustained us all. For just a little while I enjoyed the possibility of having a delicate name that meant water lily, but I had to face reality. Names were passed on from ancestors to relatives. It was unheard of to give a name from a different family or group of relatives. Names generally stayed within the bloodline.

No one could tell me anything more so I pictured Dad's aunt Nk'xetko as a hardworking woman who had rough gnarled hands from splitting cedar roots and weaving baskets, tanning deer hides and slicing meat and fish. My parents didn't press the matter, and I strongly felt they wanted me to pursue further education rather than place a lot of value on a name's meaning.

GRADE SEVEN AT SCHOOL — 1963

I enjoyed learning about the Assyrian Empire in grade seven history. Lamassu, the winged bull, piqued my interest, but the Assyrian kings sounded like merciless dictators, sacking civilizations with mighty armies and ruling with iron fists. I wondered how everyday citizens, and especially children my age, lived under this oppression. Did they have hopes and dreams?

I regretted that our ancestors' history was never mentioned in school. They lived on the land for hundreds of years before Europeans arrived, yet this was omitted from the history books.

After school we had freedom for an hour before the supper bell rang. We could go outside for a walk or stay in the rec rooms to play cards, listen to the radio, or play board games such as checkers or monopoly. After supper we had to go back to our classrooms to get homework completed for the next day. After that it was time to get ready for bed at 9 p.m.

Come grade seven, we could attend school dances. We danced with boys in the gym to the latest songs of the hit parade. If someone broke school rules, they lost that privilege. Dances were held several times throughout the year. Staying alone in the dorm while everyone else was out socializing was a punishment. Putting on a nice dress, curling our hair and dancing with a guy who caught our eye almost made us forget where we were, a strict institution. Holding hands, hugging, kissing or dancing more than twice with the same person was strictly forbidden. The nuns patrolled couples on the dance floor and thwarted displays of affection. The home waltz was the main event; guys asked their favourite girls to dance and acted dejected when the song came to an end.

At one Hallowe'en dance, Sister Cleo appeared in her infamous gorilla mask, broom in hand. This sent all of us girls screaming into the arms of the boys, who seemed to enjoy their new duties as protectors. Hugs and handholding took place sneakily amid the chaos. Sister Cleo came face-to-face with a big guy and raised her broom to swat him, but he caught the handle mid-air in an iron grip. They stared each other in the eye until she relented and scurried off. The gorilla mask never made an appearance at another dance. Watching Sister meet her match was the unexpected highlight of the evening.

Sister Cleo found other less obvious ways to vex us though. As I lay sick in bed one day, I heard her enter her room nearby. She carried an electric kettle in one hand, and I recognized the stamped envelopes of our outgoing letters and mail in the other. In the quietude of the dorm, I could hear paper rustling after the kettle of water had boiled. I realized she was steaming open the envelopes and reading our mail. I was furious and decided to write Mom with my usual greetings, but in the Ntle'kepmx language. Next time I saw Mom I asked if she got my letter. She just grinned and nodded.

"Did you understand my writing?" I asked

"Yes."

I knew how to write in English, but not in our language, so my words were slightly jumbled, but Mom got the main points and acted pleased with my effort.

"Why didn't you write back to me?" I demanded.

Again, she just grinned and didn't say anything. Sister Cleo never scolded me for this transgression, as it would have forced her to reveal that she regularly invaded our privacy.

Although fleeting, I still saw my siblings around school. One day at recess, Austin ran up to me and opened his fist to reveal a pile of coins totaling ninety-two cents. He explained that a boy named Lenny Jackson gave him money to tell me that he liked me. I wanted to take those coins and throw them away.

I summoned my angriest voice and yelled, "I DO NOT LIKE HIM. Tell him that!"

Austin grinned, turned and trotted away. A few weeks later, I asked him if he passed my message on to Lenny.

"Nah," he said. "I just spent the money on candy."

While home later that year for Easter holidays I asked Ya-yeh to teach me to make a pair of buckskin moccasins. She patiently helped me cut out the pattern, stitch the pieces together and embroider flowers on for the finishing touch. It was a success, I felt so elated with my work and wore the *'sil'stu'uy* moccasins proudly. Ya-yeh appeared pleased with me too.

Nema shi esh: "That is good," she said.

I witnessed Ya-yeh one time walking in the field alone. She gestured with her hands as though speaking with someone. I asked Mom who she was speaking with. "She speaks with the Creator and tells everything that concerns her."

I was amazed at the different way praying was enforced on us at school. We had to kneel on our knees for long periods of time to repeat fifty Hail Mary's in saying 'the rosary'. Sometimes our knees became numb.

SUMMER — 1964

A travel agent in Kamloops arranged for our dance troupe to fly to Mexico City to put on two performances. That meant living at the residential school in July to prepare for the trip. To cover airfare plus hotel, we sought donations by putting on local performances. Kamloops citizens happily helped us out. Parents and friends of the dancers gladly gave donations, too, for our trip of a lifetime. We practiced the Mexican song "Cielito Lindo" until our voices were hoarse.

The idea had sprung when a visiting group of singers and musicians from Vera Cruz, the Talavera Brothers performed in town and at the school. They caused a sensation with their harmonious voices accompanied by guitar, harp and maracas. We put on a show of our dances for them. They promised that if we made it to Mexico, they would be glad to host us. That's all we could think of during those months. We could hardly contain our excitement and anticipation. For the first time, it felt worthwhile to be a dancer.

St. Mary's Indian Residential School in Mission City had a marching band whose members wore white moccasins and white outfits trimmed with brown fringe. We borrowed these to wear in public, in addition to our standard uniform which consisted of a red blazer, grey skirt and white blouse. We were each permitted to bring a small suitcase and no more than twenty dollars spending money. We spent the seven-hour Canadian Airlines flight giddy with excitement repeating phrases, "Buenos dias, Señor," and "Gracias mi amigo." Upon arrival that evening at the airport someone took pictures, flashbulbs glittered causing more excitement.

Every minute in Mexico brought something new and magical. Our guides shared history and facts as they ushered us onto buses destined for the pyramids, museums and even to the Floating Gardens of Xochimilco. We put on a show at Arena Mexico for an audience of several thousand people. They nearly shook the building down with applause at the finish. Our other performance took place at the Palace of Fine Arts for a smaller, less boisterous crowd. In the middle of a duet, Shirley's dance partner got a leg cramp and limped offstage. Shirley carried on alone, completing the number to a thunderous ovation.

Between rehearsals, tours and photo ops, we visited open-air markets, a palace and other historic locales. We were treated more like ambassadors than young performers because the money generated from our performances went to help out various causes such as the rehabilitation centre. At one market I picked out a leather wallet with the Aztec calendar design when the cashier, a young man offered to give it to me for free because he liked the color of my eyes. Shirley overheard, tossed the wallet back and dragged me out of there with a warning,

"Be careful around men. Nothing is free. He's a wolf in sheep's clothing."

I found another wallet and purchased it for two pesos and didn't linger around men anymore. Apparently, some men can't be trusted around girls. It was a lesson to remember.

A bus brought us to the silver town of Taxco. I was dazzled by the gems imbedded in silver bracelets, rings and pendants. For five pesos I purchased a wristband with blue carved faces and felt very pleased with such a colorful memento. We headed to Acapulco for a few days of rest, but I refused to swim in the ocean because I'd heard there were sharks in the water. We were feeling sad to be departing from such friendly and hospitable people, but we also felt happy to be going home to family and familiar surroundings. Despite their best efforts, many of our troupe contracted the dreaded "mala tourista" at a local restaurant. Pain and suffering of stomach flu for a few days dampened our travel fun.

I had borrowed my brother Robert's camera and, when we returned to Kamloops, I paid $2.83 to develop the photos I took during that memorable trip. Back at Joeyaska, my family enjoyed looking at the photos, despite my lackluster photography skills.

Mexico became a distant memory. A package arrived for me from Mexico. Alfredo, the young man assigned to take our pictures sent me a few photos and asked to correspond with me. I hadn't taken notice of him at all, had no idea who he was. His photos were much better than mine. He caused me to feel pretty and special, so we wrote to each other for about a year, then it tapered off. Life and homework, school and boys took over my world.

GRADE EIGHT AT SCHOOL — 1964

Dad dropped us off at the front of the school building on Labour Day weekend. Shirley went to the annex, a new building for the high school students, and Austin left for the boys' side. This was to be the first year our dance troupe was disbanded. No more practices, performances, no more being yelled at. It was a liberating feeling. I headed off to see who my new supervisor was in the intermediate rec room. I walked alone down the long, empty hallway, looking grown-up in my new jacket, stirrup pants and Beatle boots. The place was quiet, but Sister Kay was at her desk. She stood when she saw me.

"You Sterling's think you're so smart," she said, her mouth curling in a sneer.

I groaned silently and willed Dad to show up and rescue me. It was pretty clear what kind of school year it was going to be. She yanked my hair when checking for nits and pointed to my old locker, number 142. I knew the routine: I put my suitcase in the Linen Room, locked up my money, and collected my flannel nightgown, towels and sheets. She assigned me a bed on the fourth-floor dorm near her room. Another silent groan as visions of Sister Kay barking orders at us like an army captain danced through my head.

We were allowed to wear our own clothes after school, so we kept favorite items in our lockers, hoping no thieves stole our favorite things, there were no locks on the doors. My sisters gave me their clothes and sometimes other girls liked to borrow a blouse or skirt. There was an emphasis on "no short skirts allowed." We had to always dress modestly.

We received our work assignments the following day. These were chores that each student completed every morning after breakfast throughout the school year. In front of the group, Sister Kay assigned me to the toilets. She seemed to relish giving me the least desirable of all tasks. I didn't mind. There was no choice in the matter anyway.

Tidying up the sacristy after the priests finished saying mass in the chapel was the most prized job, but it came with strict orders:

"Do not eat the hosts or drink the wine." A few months into the school year, the girl assigned to the sacristy got caught doing just that. She was demoted to the toilets and, though it pained Sister Kay, I was given sacristy duty.

"I don't want to choose you," she said, pulling me from the crowd, "but I know you won't eat the hosts or drink the wine."

"Yes, Sister," I replied, masking my elation with a serious expression.

My classmate, Gladys, was once caught holding hands with a boy named Bill in a dark corner outside. Sister Kay called me and Gladys over to a quiet spot and ordered me to keep her away from Bill. I resented having to chaperone a girl my own age, but I couldn't refuse. Gladys had attitude and often ran away from me to go see Bill. I'd catch up, steer her away and escort her to and from class. She gave up on being mean and nasty, so I let her talk to Bill when no one was looking. We didn't become friends, but we got along peaceably.

One morning at breakfast I found a large white grub in my cornmeal. I stared at it aghast and couldn't eat. When Sister Kay came by, I showed it to her. She glared at me and said,

"Eat your porridge and be thankful." She stood staring at me for a long time as I gagged down small amounts. She finally walked away. A girl nearby wanted my bowlful because she was hungry. We weren't allowed to throw food away, we had to eat every scrap.

When the Christmas concert rolled around, I was surprised to see my brother Robert grinning in the audience. As our grade eight class walked on stage to perform, Sister Kay pulled me from the group and shoved me to the front to introduce our number. I tripped and stumbled, catching hold of the microphone. Later, I asked Robert if he saw me on stage.

"Oh yeah, Chur-chur," he said, using the nickname he had for me. "You put on a performance all by yourself."

My siblings and I collected our suitcases and joined Robert in the parlour, where he sat waiting. As we marched out the front doors past a large statue of St. Ann, Robert poked two fingers into the statue's eyeballs. Contrary to my expectations, he wasn't struck down on the spot, and we sped off toward Joeyaska.

I later learned that Robert had visited a girl on the Kamloops reserve and offered to pick us up in his new car on the way home. His job paid well, and for Christmas he bought Shirley and me new leather boots lined with sheep wool to keep our feet warm. The school issued everyone rubber boots to wear over our shoes in the winter, but these didn't stand up to ice and snow. On chilly days, my feet toasty warm, I thought of Robert's kindness.

Back at school in January, Saturday was laundry day. I pressed sheets and pillowcases on a machine called a mangle, alongside Sister Kay. She was working at the extractor machines, which wrung out wet clothes from the washer. Everyone else was gone, and we were alone. One of the machines came to a noisy, clanging halt.

"You broke this machine!" Sister Kay yelled at me.

"No, I didn't!" I responded instinctively, not thinking.

I broke the rule by talking back. The machine was ten feet away from me; she knew I hadn't contributed to its failure but seemed to need to blame someone, me. Her face turned red.

"I said you broke this machine," she retorted, "so you broke it."

This time, I didn't reply, fear dissolving my memory of whatever happened next.

I wasn't the only student Sister Kay picked on. Later that school year, she bellowed at Maxine, a tough, no-nonsense girl who wasn't afraid of anyone. We stayed away from her for our own safety. Maxine had broken some rule. Sister Kay lifted her fist to hit Maxine, but she was too slow. Maxine ducked and pulled off Sister Kay's veil. We all gasped to see brown hair in a short brush cut. Sister Kay grabbed the veil and quickly restored it to her head, but not before her face turned scarlet and we glimpsed her vulnerability.

"No Friday night movies for one month, Maxine Bob!" screamed Sister Kay.

We saw Maxine smirk and turn away. She didn't care. We wanted to applaud her bravery, and we would have if we didn't fear the same punishment.

Grade eight girls took home economics, and we learned cooking from the meanest nun in the school, Sister Morna. She assigned me a curried rice recipe. Whenever I get scared, I forget what to do, so, in my panic, I hadn't heard the instruction to cut the recipe in half. Not only did I prepare a whole pot of curried rice, I burned it. Thereafter, I became known as the girl who burned rice, and I was on the receiving end of many scowls from Sister Morna.

In addition to cooking, we learned French. We already heard another language in our homes, so many of us picked up French quite easily.

"Here's the future French teacher," Sister Deloras said to me often, her encouragement buoying me during an otherwise tumultuous year.

In literature class, our assignment in May was to write a short poem about our mothers. It was easy for me. I wrote:

> "Mom, you are a fragrant rose in the garden.
> Thorns are your hard times.
> Your beauty is like a blossom.
> I am happy when I see you. Your beauty is like a
> blossom. I am happy when I see you."

After that we put together letters for our mothers along with the poems and mailed them. One stamp cost five cents. Another class assignment was to compose a letter for our dads. My mind went blank. I didn't know how to write a note to someone like Dad. That was something I noticed about the difference in communication. Dad and Mom spoke in their languages for hours with others, but they spoke only minimal sentences to us their children in the English language.

In English class, one day I sat in the front row listening to Sister Batista deliver a pronunciation lesson, droplets of her spittle landing on my face. Someone behind whispered my name, and I turned to look. Sister Batista slapped me hard, I almost fell out of my desk. I saw stars, and it took me a while to regain my bearings. Shortly after that incident my name went up on the honour roll for high marks, but this didn't erase the shame I felt. Someone snapped a photo of the eight of us honour roll students; in it, I look crestfallen.

I thought about this controlled environment at the residential school. To say that I hated it would be an understatement. We couldn't have opinions, nor disagree with the nuns or priests. We were forced to suppress our feelings at all times. I was convinced we were expected to grow up to become empty headed robots.

This was different from our family's teachings which allowed us to learn by watching, then do for ourselves. We could make a mistake with only a reminder to do better next time as opposed to a scolding. Dad could be quite harsh though: "Don't you grow up to be useless," he'd say. That prompted me to try and be careful.

Grade eight was difficult because of Sister Kay. One day during free time everyone was relaxing in the rec room. Sister Kay called me out to clean and dust the linen room closets and mop the floor. I was tired and even sweating a little upon finishing up, so when I went in to join the other girls I sat down. Instantly Sister Kay assigned another task to me, and because I sat there and didn't get up immediately, she said pointing to me,

"Some of you are so lazy, the dirt will fall off you."

Inwardly I groaned, and didn't even understand her words. I could see my classmates looking at me with pity as I walked out to do the next job. I wondered why she didn't ask anyone else. I was sweating because I worked fast to get the job done. I didn't want to be alone in a room with Sister Kay. I felt afraid of her.

My sister Sarah had experienced the harshness of Sister Kay years earlier. Once when Sarah talked with Hector in the supper line up, Sister Kay grabbed Sarah, flipped her to the floor and stepped on her neck and told her,

"You are going to become a prostitute if you continue flirting with boys."

At the end of the school year our grade eight PE classes merged for a mixed boys and girls baseball game on the field. I couldn't bat the ball nor run fast, but catching pop flies for my brothers paid off. During this game I was placed out at center field. One of the boys batted the ball up and out. I heard the comment, "She's too dainty – she'll never catch that." I caught that ball easily, and silenced the nasty comments. Our team didn't win, but we gained new respect from the boys.

SUMMER — 1965

The school principal, Father Francis, arranged waitress training for me and my friend Bev in July. Someone from the school drove us to the training course in Kamloops and picked us up every day. The instructor found us a one-month position at the Sand and Sage Hotel and Cafe in Ashcroft, BC. We waited tables, made milkshakes, helped the cook, cleaned rooms and generally kept busy. Bev was a beautiful girl, and she had to fend off the attentions of every guy who came through that summer. She generated lots of business for the café, I'd heard. Guys from near and far came in and enjoyed teasing us young girls. I didn't appreciate it because I became flustered and usually forgot part of their order which resulted in no tips for me.

When the pubs closed after nine in the evenings, several patrons came to the café. Many of them ordered large plates of chop suey and fried rice with their pork dishes. Big spenders asked for T-Bone steaks cooked medium rare. These customers were generally in jolly moods and left us big tips when the bills were paid, then off they went into the night.

On our days off, we explored the town, there wasn't too much to see. One day we went inside the Anglican church to check if it was any different than Catholic churches. It looked the same, but we felt like we broke some kind of unwritten rule and got out of there in a hurry. On one occasion, we visited a gal named Joan from Merritt who had married a cowboy and moved to the Bonaparte reserve, past Cache Creek. She raised her children, helped run the ranch, and tended to her horses and garden. She picked us up along the highway one day, took us to her home, fed us a tasty meal then brought us back to the hotel. It was the highlight of our summer in Ashcroft.

A note was shoved into my hand during a busy time. On reading it later I was surprised. I had no idea who the guy was, it read,

"Come away with me to Tacoma, Washington. I'm a race car driver. You're too good for this town. Signed, Jerry Bruhn." I was fifteen years old, looked twelve. It puzzled me to the core. It was a message that caused fear in me. I didn't know how I invited that kind of attention. I was taught to be prim and proper as a teen, and not to look for attention from guys.

When our jobs finished, we caught the bus back to Kamloops, opened bank accounts, deposited our cheques and headed home to Merritt. Bev was a good workmate, she was reliable and hardworking, pleasant and agreeable, a dear friend. After parting ways I was glad for a chance to catch up with my own family for a time before school started in September. This meant picking huckleberries in the mountains, camping out and enjoying homegrown food. I had eaten so many hamburgers in Ashcroft, I couldn't touch ground beef for years to come.

I recall in one of our quiet times together Bev told me about how her cousin Sam described some nights at the residential school He said men with flashlights came into the boys dorm, their breath smelled of alcohol.

"What do you think they were doing," she asked.

I was dumbfounded and had no idea. We could only shake our heads in disbelief.

GRADE NINE AT SCHOOL — 1965

When my parents dropped me off at residential school in September, I felt more grown up at age fifteen. Shirley had graduated and moved on. It was my turn to live in the annex for grade nine, the newer dorm. It was such an improvement over the old building which had cramped quarters, creaking stairs and long hallways that smelled of disinfectant. The annex housed ten bedrooms on the second floor. Each bedroom had beds, night tables and lockers for six students. There were new bathrooms and showers, and two large study rooms with sofas and tables in the basement—one for the boys, one for us. So modern and spacious. A locked and bolted double-door separated the boys' side from the girls' side of the school. The boy's dorm was located on the first floor. It was off limits to us girls, and our dorm on the second floor was off limits to them.

Sister Morna awaited our arrival, her lips pulled tight and her eyes narrowed in a glare. We knew all about her from grade eight home economics, and many girls called her "Sister Witch" behind her back. Shirley was under her care the previous year. Shirley was a talented dancer who was given permission by the school principal to pursue ballet at a studio in Kamloops. Father Parant took it upon himself to drive Shirley to and from dance practice. Just once I got to see her "toe shoes" as she demonstrated her pointe. It looked painful, but I admired her persistence. As a result of ballet practice, she was often late for other duties, resulting in the scolding wrath of Sister Morna.

"Of all the nuns, try to avoid Sister Morna," she told me, "I barely survived her cruelty."

Our routines were the same as ever, but we had a television in the rec room. CBC was the only channel, and in winter we watched hockey. Some of us were great fans of the Canadian teams, influenced by our dads and older brothers. My brothers cheered for Frank Mahovlich of the Toronto Maple Leafs. When I watched the game, I knew my brothers watched the same game elsewhere, those moments helped me feel close to them.

My new roommates were from the Lillooet and Chase areas. They talked of their homelife and favourite songs on the radio, which generally coincided with what boy they liked or had just broken up with. I enjoyed their company. We commiserated about our studies and the rigours of finding oneself on Sister Morna's bad side. "Stay out of her way" was the rule of the day. Don't make eye contact. We found things to laugh about, humour helped us survive the rough times. "You think Sister Morna ever smiles?" brought a chuckle now and then.

We were not allowed to think of ourselves as pretty, or smart or talented. The nuns didn't allow that kind of thinking, we heard them say,

"We'll bring you down a notch."

Mom had also attended Kamloops Indian Residential School in 1923 and described being whipped for speaking our language. One time I asked her how she got over the cruelty.

"I wrote a letter to *Oła kwuk pi*, the High Chief. I wrote about the beatings and asked him to forgive Sister Malachi."

She related how she burned the letter afterward and let it all go. I doubted I could be as forgiving as I stared into her eyes wondering if she

was really telling the truth. We had come a long way in this modern era of education. We were punished for infractions, but life was easier when you spoke English. Mom gave me the courage to carry on.

Grade nine meant "integration" into a Catholic high school in Kamloops. We were bussed across the river, through town and up to St. Ann's Academy. The Department of Indian Affairs offered to build a new classroom at any public or private school that would take us, and St. Ann's had risen to the occasion.

The transition from isolated villages brought culture shock for many of my classmates. Some of them ran away and were never heard from again. It was the first time I met white people. They were different from us. Their middle-class sensibilities made me feel self-conscious and inferior. But my older sisters had graduated from St. Ann's and assured me that the school provided a good foundation for university. Dad wouldn't allow us to drop out of school anyway, except for Sarah who eloped. We had no choice but to endure the hardships of study, persevere to final exams and go on to bigger and better dreams.

The president of St. Ann's student council was interviewed one day on the local Kamloops television channel. When asked about the Native students attending St. Ann's, she described us as "nothing but a bunch of snobs." Silently I wondered if she could tell us that to our faces. I knew that we came from communities where the roads weren't paved, there was no indoor plumbing and kerosene lamps or lanterns lit our homes at night. We were shy.

Sister Joyce used the "new math" method, popularized in the fifties and sixties, to teach us mathematics. She delivered her classes in a monotone voice, which sometimes lulled me to sleep. The concepts were lost on me, I failed that course and was advised to repeat it the following year. Thankfully, only grade eleven mathematics was required for university entrance, which allowed me to dodge summer school.

During baseball's World Series in October, Sister Joyce closed the books and turned the radio on so we could all listen in class. I liked baseball. My brothers played on different teams in Merritt, and they occasionally held batting practice in the fields. I liked to run and collect the baseballs for them. They paid me one dollar each to wash and press their team uniforms.

NEW YEARS EVE AT HOME

I was growing up and, during winter break that year, I attended my first New Year's Eve dance with my older sisters. We stood in front of the only mirror in our home, which was located in the kitchen, combing our hair and putting on lipstick.

"Hey, not too much lipstick!" Dad said. "Wash some of that off. You don't want them guys looking at you like that."

We pretended not to hear him and off we went in somebody's car.

I planned to meet up with a young man from a nearby reserve. He was sober and handsome, and I enjoyed his company. The dance started out tame, but as the night wore on things started to get out of hand. By midnight, fights were breaking out. The tone changed when the countdown began though. Everyone settled down and kissed each other politely at the stroke of midnight. Kissing strangers did not appeal to me. My sisters arranged a ride home for us, so I said goodnight to my date. I told him he'd have to get past my dad if he wanted to see me again; perhaps that frightened him because he never tried. I was not impressed by the way alcohol changed people's behaviour in negative ways at what was supposed to be a fun event.

SISTER BEVERLY MITCHELL

At St. Ann's Academy, my homeroom teacher, Sister Beverly, loved literature. Her enthusiasm was contagious, and I looked forward to returning to her lessons after winter break. She once gave our class an hour to write a poem entitled *Thoughts on Silence*. I didn't know what to write, so I gazed out the window, thoughts turning to Mom and home life. How I longed for family and all the familiar sights and sounds that warmed my heart. Being away at school was very lonely.

"Three minutes left. Finish up your poem," said Sister Beverly, pulling me from my reverie.

I said a quick prayer, asking for divine writing inspiration. In three minutes, I frantically penned an eighteen-line poem about the very things I had daydreamed about. Sister Beverly loved my work so much she sent it to an editor named Kent Gooderham, who was compiling the first book of Indigenous peoples' writings from across Canada. It was entitled *I Am an Indian*. When the book was published two years later, I received $100 and a copy of the book. I was dumbfounded but happily deposited the money into my bank account. I recall Sister hadn't even asked me about submitting my work. That's what was so surprising.

The month of May meant graduation and prom time. I was in grade nine, and Father Francis assigned me to accompany a young man who had completed grade twelve but was too shy to ask anyone out. I had no choice in the matter. Sister found me a pink dress to wear. Someone combed my hair into a French roll, and I borrowed a pair of white sandals. My classmates teasingly referred to me as Cinderella.

In the decorated gym, everyone was glowing, joyful and beautifully dressed. But there I was, sitting silently with a guy whose only words to me were, "Want a glass of punch?" At the end of that long evening, I informed him that we had to dance the home waltz. Neither of us were any good. I felt awkward and clumsy, out of place. Then, mercifully, it was over. It was an experience that can only be described as uncomfortable.

I never understood the concept of getting dressed up to dance in the gym. Our people had a different way of celebrating that included drumming and singing ancestral songs in our language. Mom told me of going late at night as a youngster for drum songs and dance at a home with blacked-out windows to partake of ceremony in secret because of the laws restricting the practice of our culture. White society treated us like we were on the lowest rung on the racial hierarchy, so putting on fancy clothes to pretend we were acceptable felt farcical. Like trying something on that you knew was two sizes too big or too small and being forced to wear it.

At the end of the school year in June Father Parant planned to drive to the Merritt area to say Sunday mass in the local churches, so he gave a few of us students a ride home. He must have phoned ahead to my parents because he dropped Austin and I off at a new house. It had just recently been completed in one of the lower fields of the ranch beside the Coldwater road. I didn't know about this change. No one told me. What a surprise to have electricity and running water, indoor plumbing. Mom still had a wood stove to cook on, and there was a phone on the wall. Father Parant appeared pleased to be part of the surprise. He drove away grinning and waving at us.

Robert had gotten married and wanted our old house. That was the arrangement. I quickly found out the phone numbers of my friends. Our moms had already contacted each other. Everything was so new, and different, it took getting used to. For the first time my home felt modern and new. The only thing I missed was the corral and barn where the horses were kept. To go riding meant a trek across the fields. I couldn't lift a saddle, so often I just rode bareback, happy to be on my homeland seeing familiar sights. It looked and felt peaceful.

Fred had taken over running the ranch so Dad had more free time. At this time Sarah had to go to the cancer clinic in Vancouver for treatment. Her three sons stayed with my parents who gladly welcomed them. Dad appeared happy with the children, he purchased chocolate bars to hand out to his grandsons everyday. I noticed them following Dad around the ranch while he completed minor chores.

GRADE TEN AT SCHOOL — 1966

Each high school class at St. Ann's elected leaders to learn responsibility, representation and the intricacies of how government ran. I was nominated for class secretary and won. This role required me to sit in on monthly meetings with the class representatives while the principal looked on. It was an eye-opener. I recorded concerns raised by the students, intrigued to note that everyone seemed to have a voice which was respected, unlike being a status Indian with no say, no consultation whatsoever. The Department of Indian Affairs made decisions for us, attempting to raise us to the level of democracy. We needed to get through the education system first, which seemed complicated by language barriers, separation from family and enforced assimilation. It appeared to be a tangled web of bureaucracy.

My nephew Greg attended the residential school for first grade. A bully on the boy's side pushed him down the stairs. Greg was taken to the hospital with a broken ankle. Austin and I were allowed to go visit him. I felt very sad that I couldn't do anything to protect him. After the school year finished Greg attended school elsewhere. Hopefully to a safer environment.

During Christmas holidays Mom helped me pick out some fabric at the shop to make a pink and white lace dress. I planned to wear it to my first Valentine Dance at St. Ann's Academy and I wanted it to be special. We followed the pattern and sewed it together and felt very pleased with the finished result. We rarely could afford to buy new clothes. Sewing was a pleasant alternative where Mom was an expert and I picked up on her clever techniques.

After Christmas, it was time to fundraise again. St. Ann's being an independent school was always looking for money to help cover costs. For the Valentine Dance, one penny could cast a vote for a King or Queen of

Hearts. Father Francis heard about the fundraiser and donated a couple of hundred dollars in coins to the cause in my name. I was only in grade ten when I was declared the Queen of Hearts at St. Ann's due to the generosity of Father Francis (who probably liked getting rid of all those loose coins). The king was a handsome Italian fellow, but we had nothing in common and didn't speak to one another. We sat quietly, relieved when our official duty ended. Everyone else seemed to have fun stepping lively to the music. A dance at school seemed to be a type of celebration, staff and teachers held it over us to behave if we wanted to attend.

I didn't attend any other school dances at St. Ann's. I didn't feel comfortable socializing with the students. Our backgrounds were too different. Besides, asking Brother Pike for a ride to St. Ann's was asking for blame and accusation to be heaped on us by an angry, bitter driver. We already felt bad enough about ourselves.

EXTRA CURRICULAR ACTIVITIES AT SCHOOL

Our teacher, Sister Magrite, held poetry readings in class to choose a few of us to compete in the district competitions. She picked me to read a short poem by Robert Frost. I practiced and memorized stanzas, adding emphasis on imagery changes. When the day came to recite in front of the judges, every one of us performed very well. My voice was quiet, and I received a certificate of merit for placing third. It was good practice to face an audience.

I joined choir as well. Practice during noon hours helped quicken the monotony of school routine. And when a marching band was formed for the high school girls at the residential school, I signed up. I didn't read music but played the trumpet with three others; we listened to a song and could play it by ear. It was a drum and bugle band. My older sisters advised me to join different activities to make the time pass by quickly. They were right.

Shortly thereafter, my brother Fred's basketball team in Merritt challenged our school team to a friendly game on a Saturday afternoon. My sister Sarah came, and we sat together catching up. My only news was being elected Queen of Hearts, one penny per vote.

"Oh, your sisters were chosen as Queen of Hearts years ago," she said, laughing. "You kept the tradition!"

She told me that when Deanna was elected Queen of Hearts, she was so surprised she couldn't speak at the microphone but stood staring in silence.

I realized that there was a lot I didn't even know about my own family. We seemed to be disconnected from each other, occasionally coming together, only to drift apart again. Dad stressed self-sufficiency and, as we grew up, we cast off in search of independence.

Our girls' basketball team was challenged to a match by St. Mary's Indian Residential School in Mission. We travelled in our yellow bus to

Mission and stayed in the girls' dorm, doubling up in beds. I slept on my side, not moving an inch all night so as not touch my bedmate. It was awkward to wake up stiff in the morning. Our team needed support, so three of us rose to the occasion to cheerlead. We wore long yellow and green pleated skirts that hit below our knees, saddle oxfords, white socks, and we shook crepe paper pompoms.

"Two, four, six, eight," we cheered, "Who do you appreciate? Go... Kamloops!"

St. Mary's team was skilled, and the game ended in a tie. At the dance that followed, I sat quietly until a dashing young man named Wayne, who reminded me of the movie star Warren Beatty, came over. I liked his company; he had a sense of humour and could converse on any topic. We exchanged addresses and agreed to write to each other. He lived on the Musqueam reserve near Vancouver, and we promised to keep in touch. The next morning, we boarded the bus to depart. Wayne and his aunt stood grinning at me, eyes twinkling in some mysterious mischief as they waved goodbye. Our next visit was to Stanley Park and the Vancouver Aquarium, to enjoy a picnic lunch packed by the cooks at St. Mary's.

Being at the annex meant decent food probably because we were a smaller group, seventy-five of us grades nine to twelve. A treat on Friday's was a breakfast of scrambled eggs, toast and hot cocoa. The cooks prepared sandwiches, cookies and fruit for our school lunches at St. Ann's. We appreciated their efforts and let them know by saying thank you every day.

Back at school, our supervisor Sister Ellen's old-fashioned ways were weighing on the girls. When we went for long walks, she made us walk two by two. In our free time, she pushed us to embroider, as we imagined a nineteenth-century governess would have done. The girls pushed back and wouldn't comply.

Worse than Sister Ellen's antiquated ways, though, was the underlying disdain she had for her pupils.

"They're nothing but a bunch of dirty Indians," she and another nun complained loudly.

It's possible they didn't know we'd overheard, or perhaps they just didn't care. Whichever the case, after that, many girls treated her rudely. By the end of the school year, she fell ill and was sent to recover in a convalescent home. For some reason none of us felt sorry for her.

SUMMER AT HOME — 1967

Expo 67 was taking place in Montreal, and it would be the first time Native Canadian art was featured for the world to see. We were starved for our art and culture at school. We knew who we were, but Canada generally ignored us—at best—and made us feel inferior, at worst.

However, each July 1ˢᵗ, Canada Day our family joined many other Ntle'kepmx and townsfolk at Voght Park, south of Merritt. It was a time of relaxing, visiting and sharing picnic lunches. There was a parade, a bingo game and foot races. One year I was invited to help Mabel Joe and her family decorate a float for the parade celebrating Ntle'kepmx culture. My brother Fred offered his truck and a flat deck trailer. We cut bull rushes, tied them on, displayed our basketry and dressed the children in buckskin clothing. Robert's wife loaned me her buckskin dress so I could dance on the trailer with my friend Judy while elder Louis John drummed a song. We were happy to participate in a positive and celebratory event. Our float came in second place.

I wanted a summer job to earn money to travel to Montreal, but nothing materialized. One day I was riding JW Baldy when Austin arrived home with Dad, mail in hand. He waved a letter at me that was postmarked from Vancouver. I was overjoyed, assuming it was from Wayne. I manoeuvred the horse as close as possible to the door to avoid wasting the time it would take to jump off.

"You might as well ride the horse right into the house while you're at it," said Austin, handing me the letter.

Still in the saddle, I read Wayne's letter with glee, admiring his neat handwriting and politeness. In the end, neither of us had much to report. He lived in the city, I lived in the country. I was entering grade eleven, he was entering grade twelve. We had little in common and, after I replied to his letter, our correspondence fizzled.

A letter from Shirley also arrived for me. She had married a man named Reinhard and was living on Vancouver Island. She invited me for a two-week holiday to help alleviate her loneliness. She outlined all the information I needed to get there:

"It's $8.00 from Kamloops to Vancouver, then $4.00 to Nanaimo and $3.00 to Port Alberni," she wrote. "We can pick you up by boat there and bring you to Bamfield. Phone Peter Jantis at 19A, he lives next door, it will cost 25 cents..."

My parents agreed to give me bus fare and a bit of spending money. The trip, which turned out to be smooth sailing, took one day by bus. I arrived in Port Alberni that night and slept in their sailboat turned fishing boat. Fishing was poor (that's why they were so broke), but I loved hiking in the forests, swimming in the ocean and picnicking on the beaches. Shirley made sure I had a fun, memorable time.

A cute teenage boy lived nearby. He thought I was twelve years old, likely deceived by my pigtails. By the time I revealed I was sixteen, it was too late; it was time to return home to Merritt for our family's summer rituals.

Camping in the mountains was always the highlight of my life. That was where I could relax and just enjoy the berries, the fresh air and time with the people I loved.

GRADE ELEVEN AT SCHOOL — 1967

My friend and I got the job of cleaning the principal's room, a task only the most trustworthy were given. Feeling mischievous, we decided to play a prank on Father Francis, the new school's principal. It was called a "French bed" and entailed folding the sheets in half to prevent the person from climbing into the bed. Father Francis was easygoing and had a good sense of humour, so we thought he'd enjoy it. However, Sister Superior heard about it and felt otherwise. She grounded us from movie nights for one month, eliciting tears from both me and my accomplice. Father Francis called us over and forgave us, laughing at the whole episode. Noticing our tearstained cheeks, he instructed Sister to forego punishing our innocent childhood shenanigans.

At St. Ann's, we had Sister Beverly again for English class. She played a recording of Leonard Cohen singing "Suzanne," a song about a free spirit living in a boat near the river in Quebec. She explained that the words of the song held deeper meaning than what was apparent on the surface; she asked us to let our imaginations take us to a realm beyond. The exercise was lost on me, but I liked the music, and anything that displaced lectures was a gift.

Before we went home for Christmas holidays, Sister Beverly asked me and my two classmates from Merritt to gather knowledge about our ancestors for a class presentation. She requested a legend, facts about our culture such as food, clothing and shelter, a song, and a dance. My parents cautiously complied, providing the information I required. When Mom and Dad attended residential school, they were brutally punished for speaking in their language, and all cultural knowledge was forbidden in their classrooms. A few of their school mates were whipped until they passed out. It appeared that education was meant to beat our culture out of us, a notion that lingered in the minds of my parents' generation.

"When the priests punished you, they meant to cripple you," Dad told us.

He endured the hardship until age fourteen when he ran away, lived in hiding until he turned sixteen at which point school attendance was no longer a Canadian law.

For the project, Dad told me a story of Coyote and the willow tree having a contest to see who could dance longer. Naturally, the willow's branches in the flowing water out-danced coyote.

Koyn chut et koyn chut et koyn chut: "He danced, and he danced, and he danced." Coyote admitted defeat. He conceded and moved along to his next adventure. Our stories meant to teach a lesson. Each listener either heard a warning or advice to be humble, not be greedy or hasty. The story was entertaining, too, filling our imaginations with visuals, sights and sounds. My mouth gaped. I was under the impression that my parents knew little of our history and culture. I began to understand that their silence was meant to protect me.

"If I didn't know my culture, I couldn't be punished for it."

Later I was brought to the Guichon Ranch at Nicola Lake to meet Okanagan elder Nellie Guiterrez, the cook. She could give me further details of Interior Salish traditions. She looked me in the eye and said, "Your great grandfather Joeyaska came from Brewster, Washington. He preempted his land in the 1870s." It was a statement that elders seemed to know. I learned later that mainly Europeans and Mexicans preempted homestead lands. Most status Indians were relegated to a reserve with five or more acres per family. Preempted lands meant lots of hard work to retain ownership.

Mom asked her friend Anna from the Coldwater reserve to make some colourful buckskin moccasins for me to wear at the presentation. I was overjoyed. Back at school, Sister asked the three of us to type out our notes so she could read them over, then she arranged a day for us to present our findings to the whole school. Interior Salish culture had never been shared in this way at St. Ann's before. Suddenly the shame that was imposed upon us for being Ntle'kepmx turned to pride in our culture—a previously foreign concept.

However, racism existed at St. Ann's. One day a blond, blue-eyed schoolmate held the door open for us three. Mockingly, with hands outstretched, he said, "Enter in, you squaws." We ignored him and put our noses in the air.

Sister Beverly's efforts went further. She signed us up to present at a cultural symposium at the University of Victoria during the Easter break. She borrowed buckskin dresses for us from Mrs. Millie Gottfriedson of the Kamloops reserve and arranged a ride with one of the teachers. The three of us girls practiced and rehearsed. We were nervous but pleased to share the wisdom of our Elders with an audience who applauded when we finished. Change seemed to be in the air, and we were delighted to be part of it. It was the single most exciting and beautiful day of my life at school. That beaded dress covered me with everything good in the world of the Ntle'kempx; my ancestry and identity truly belonged to me. I was transformed and restored to my culture. It was the first time I felt whole and complete.

I will always be grateful to Sister Beverly, who gave us the opportunity to show pride in our traditions when it had previously been denied to us. After that I no longer felt forced to conform and become a white person. I felt freedom to be myself, to be Nk'xetko. This was the first good and positive start in my school experience and Dad pressed us to stay in school.

"There is nothing for you in the town of Merritt if you quit school," he said. "And there's nothing for you here on the ranch."

It was sage advice. Schoolwork was indeed its own sort of drudgery but, as I later learned, it was an important training ground for a future of work and employment. My parents and siblings modeled discipline and independence despite some of them getting sidetracked along the way. Ultimately, they all found their paths and carried on, and I was determined to emulate their work ethic and values.

"You can't depend on anyone to look after you," they reminded me. "You have to make it on your own."

SUMMER AT HOME — 1968

I was elated to get my grade eleven report card. I passed all my subjects and had one last summer at home before starting grade twelve in the fall. I had been given a deer hide drum from the Elder who taught us songs for our presentation. He'd asked me to paint a picture on it for him, so I painted an eagle in flight. He was pleased with it. When I finished grade eleven, he gave me the drum. I was speechless. I brought it home and felt so honoured, but I didn't have a drumstick. Mom asked Ya-yeh to help me make one. Ya-yeh went to a willow bush and selected a branch. Before cutting it off, she put an offering on the ground to say thank you to the Creator for the branch that would become my drumstick. Then she cut it and peeled off the bark, fashioned a thick padding on one end, and covered it with buckskin. Her stitches were so neat and tiny, it appeared sewn by machine. She looked me in the eye and happily gave it to me, "*xe sak'min*" your drumstick. My reply, *kwuks chemx*: "Thank you."

Shortly afterward, I visited Elder Mabel Joe to ask about drum lessons. She was always generous with her knowledge and explained that the drum becomes a voice.

"If you can't sing, or speak or pray, the drum speaks to the Creator for you," she told me.

Her lesson included a steady beat for a lengthy period of time.

"We connect with our ancestors who reverenced *Oɬa kwuk pi*, the High Chief, our Creator," she said.

I cherished that information.

"Just keep asking questions," she told me. "That's the best way to learn; you'll become smart."

She made baskets, and after one of my visits she presented me with a cup and saucer made of cedar roots. It was as though she handed me medicine for all my wounds.

In August, a classmate from Merritt and I were offered jobs. Father Francis, who was always keen to see us succeed, arranged to have us live and work at the residential school for one month. We helped the cooks in the kitchen, washed dishes, did laundry and performed light housekeeping duties for visiting priests, brothers, nuns and staff. It was relaxed—pleasant even. That was because all regular staff and supervisors had gone away for the summer. In our spare time, we read library books and went for walks. Once, Father Francis invited us to watch a Hollywood movie at the drive-in theatre. The film was unremarkable, except for the leading actress' large chest.

Kwana ta tk sqomeytin "Look at her neck" I said in our language.

"I understood what you said," blurted out Father Francis, and we had a good laugh.

Occasionally, he reminded us about the French bed episode or the tears that followed. He taught us to take things in stride.

"Learn to laugh more," he said. That was easy for him to say.

Whenever my family got together, we shared comical stories, humorous events and things to make each other laugh. We never mentioned residential school.

Except one time my sister Deanna let us know that Father Parant had told her how much money was given to the school from the Government of Canada. It was sixty five cents per child per day for food.

The month flew by we enjoyed swimming in the pool in the summer. There was no one to watch us. Not like the months of June or September when our group of intermediate girls jumped in and splashed around. That was when a whole row of priests, brothers and male staff sat on chairs nearby watching us. I felt very uncomfortable, like being on display.

We earned our pay, deposited it in the bank and caught the bus home to Merritt for a few days of relaxation before school started again in September.

The Labour Day Rodeo in Merritt was a chance to visit old friends and acquaintances before heading back to school for my final year in Kamloops. I watched the events for one afternoon, then checked out the dance in the evening. A tall cowboy from Rosedale asked me to dance. He swung me around like he was calf roping. I felt like a rag doll in his calloused hands. When the music ended, I called Dad and he came to the rodeo grounds to bring me home. I could always count on Dad or anyone in our family for a ride home. I felt secure in the knowledge that I could rely on them.

As I packed my suitcase I asked Mom what she did when she and dad returned to an empty house.

"We camped in the mountains for a few days picking huckleberries to give to elders. Dad hunted deer to give to those who had no one to hunt for them. This made us feel a little better."

GRADE TWELVE AT SCHOOL — 1968

Austin enrolled in the school in Merritt, so I went alone to Kamloops that year. It felt strange and different to be the last of my family to attend the residential school. My parents dropped me off, and I entered the annex to meet my new supervisor. I did not know Sister Marcela, she sat on a small sofa in her office and patted the space beside her motioning for me to sit there. She smiled and said,

"You have to kiss me right here if you want to be one of my pets." She pointed to her face near her nose, the area close to her lip. I froze. I couldn't do it. She glared at me and brusquely issued me school clothes, towels and nightwear and delivered me to the room that I would share with other girls from Merritt. At least I would be in good company.

A couple of weeks later she handed me an envelope with my name and the school's address on it. I didn't recognize the sender. I sensed again that she didn't like me by the way she stared accusingly into my eyes. The letter was from an older man who worked in a mine in the north. He had read an article I'd written that one of my teachers submitted (without my permission) to the *Vancouver Sun* newspaper about the loss of our traditions. He was under the impression he was in love with me, so he sent me ten dollars and asked my bra size. I was horrified and showed the letter to Sister Marcela. She scolded me for seeking unwanted attention by getting my written work published.

"He's a pervert," she said. "Send that letter back to him."

I felt foolish and ashamed. I wasn't aware which essay he was referring to because my teachers never consulted me. Without telling anyone else, I held on to the letter so that on my next visit home I would burn it in the wood stove, money and all.

Two weeks into the school year, we were advised that we needed to elect a president of the high school girls. The student president would show leadership, supervise study time and take Sister Marcela's place when she was away. I was nominated but shirked from the job. After the encounter in her office, working closely with Sister Marcela didn't appeal to me. As I sat at the table, one of her pets came to me with her head held high in the air.

"You're not going to get elected," she sneered, nostrils flaring. "I'm going to win."

I didn't respond, secretly hoping she was right. On the weekend of the election, I was granted permission to return to Merritt for my cousin's wedding. I tossed the letter from that man into the wood stove and watched the purple ten dollar bill burn up in flames, hoping that was the end of that episode. When I arrived back at the annex, my classmates announced that I'd been elected president. What a predicament.

On a more positive note, I was assigned to clean Father Keely's room every weekday morning before school. His room was inside the door to the boys' side of the annex, and I felt honoured to be trusted with the task. When Father said mass at the reserve churches in the Merritt area, I was occasionally allowed to accompany him only if all my homework and assignments were completed. He was pious but friendly.

"I saw a blackbird sitting on the back of a horse in the field near the church," he related during one car ride. "I wondered if it was just resting or riding. Made me laugh. God shows me humour in nature."

A trip home once a month with a jolly priest meant time away from the tension caused by Sister Marcela. When the weather was mild, I phoned ahead and asked Dad to saddle up his horse for me to go riding. In the saddle, I felt free and in charge of my life. JW Baldy seemed to understand and no longer gave me trouble. I appreciated JW, he let me throw my arms around his neck so I could hug him and press my face into his rough mane till my heartache calmed down. Though he smelled of sweat and dust, it didn't matter. Those home visits topped me up and gave me the strength to carry on.

My role as president included taking up a collection to purchase a Christmas gift for Sister Marcela. We'd heard she wanted a goldfish, so on the final day of school at noon I walked the snowy streets of Kamloops in a freezing wind to purchase a fish. She already had a bowl, so I was able to carry the fish back to St. Ann's in a plastic bag filled with water. We all signed a card and gave her the gift which, thankfully, pleased her.

I fell ill while back in Merritt for the holidays. I had a high fever and couldn't eat anything. I slept twenty-four hours a day until Christmas, when I finally managed to sit up and have some soup made from dried salmon, as suggested by Dad. Mom placed poultices of onions and mustard on my chest and back to loosen up my lungs, after which I began to recover. One bite into a piece of dry salmon brings to memory the taste of wind and smoke and the river where my relatives catch the silvery fish in nets every summer. Sounds of knives slicing out centre bones, fins and tail, splitting the sides to dry in the hot, blazing sun amid buzzing yellow wasps immediately comes to mind. Fish eggs and dry salmon are some of our *medicine food*.

When I returned to school in January, I noticed the whites of my eyes were yellow. The school nurse brought me to the doctor in town who diagnosed me with Hepatitis A. I was quarantined for two weeks, and all the girls had to get vaccinated. I slept a lot and read Tolstoy's *War and Peace*.

Back in my room, I learned that I had been elected president of the high school girls for the second time. I was a reluctant leader but carried out my duties and eventually found my stride. I learned to relax and keep my distance from Sister Marcela and her pets. I got along with the other girls and enjoyed their company. A friend from the Skeetchestn reserve near Savona visited me in my room one time. My locker was open to reveal a piece of dry salmon on the top shelf. Maralee saw it, grabbed it and gobbled it up right away.

"Thanks, I needed that," she said.

I was speechless because that was my last piece, and I was saving it for later. It appeared we all got hungry for a taste of home. We laughed knowing how foods from the land fed our hearts and souls and brought humour into the mix. Maralee's cheerful nature was contagious. Dried salmon and deer meat reminded me of Ya-yeh, who carefully hung strips of fish and meat on her drying racks back home. She shared with anyone who stopped by to visit. Grinning, eyes twinkling, she made tea served with bannock and jam. One tasted the love and care she put into it. I savoured those pleasant memories of my family. I was hungry for the foods of home.

The Valentine's Day dance was around the corner, which meant it was time to select a Queen and King of Hearts. The girls chose a King of Hearts, and the boys chose a Queen of Hearts through secret ballot.

Votes that we held simultaneously. Through the double doors we could hear the boys cheering about something. Then Brother Miller, the boys' supervisor, knocked loudly, unlocked the double doors and popped his head in the room.

"Mary Jane Sterling" he said, the senior boys elected you as Queen of Hearts this year."

In shock, I handed him our choice for king, William Ned (a friendly young man from Douglas Lake). Runners up became the prince and princess. Many of my schoolmates cheered for me. Most of the time I felt inadequate, unqualified and lacking in courage; and yet, here were votes of support from my peers. It gave me confidence, and I was grateful for the boost and most thankful to those boys.

On the day of the dance, Sister Marcela brought us to the gym to decorate the walls with red streamers and hearts. As King and Queen of Hearts, we wore shiny crowns, sat in a place of honour and opened the evening with the first dance.

The nuns and priests looked on from the sidelines. This turned out to be my last school dance at the Kamloops Indian Residential School. Socializing at school dances gave us brief opportunities to relax and feel like normal teenagers for a change. Suddenly my final year was coming to a close. Soon I would go out into the real world. It was after this dance that Sister's pets reminded me of their hatred, saying things like,

"She thinks she's better than everyone else." There was no one to confide in. I felt depressed and discouraged wishing I could quit school or end my life somehow. I was called vain, selfish, boy-crazy and a failure by girls who didn't like me. They said it behind my back but within earshot. I felt degraded and discouraged.

MY LAST EASTER AT HOME - 1969

Over the Easter holiday, Mom presented me with a stunning buckskin jacket that she'd made for my graduation gift. It fit perfectly, and I wore it everywhere with joy. The smoked deer hide coat reminded me of my traditional culture and how Mom demonstrated her love for me. I felt very fulfilled at that time. One night I walked into Mom's bedroom, and she was so deep in prayer that she didn't hear me. I asked her the next day what she prayed about.

"I pray for my children and grandchildren. Every day. I pray you will be safe, that you will succeed in your plans."

I was very impressed with a mother who cared that much for me. No one else, no nuns, no priests ever told me that.

During the Easter break I met a young man named Matt who played baseball with my brother Fred. Matt confided that he noticed my jacket before he noticed me. He was from a reserve north of Lytton, and he worked at the copper mine southeast of Merritt. He drove a deep blue Chevy and asked to see me again. When I returned to school, we wrote to each other, getting to know one another from a distance. He was attractive, kind and considerate. I made it clear that I would head to university after graduation. He felt sad about that. I felt disappointed by the fact that he didn't consider university as a goal for his life. For the present time, his kind and gentle attention made me feel appreciated and special. I needed to hear that.

I had to visit a chiropracter over the holidays. Earlier in the school term Father Parant drove a few of us former dancers to perform at a multi-cultural function, then he left. Brother Pike was in charge of driving and picking us up from school activities. He came to get us. He was always angry and annoyed with us. To show it, he drove extra fast along the road back to the residential school. The loose gravel along the shoulder of the road caught the van's tires causing it to careen off into a ditch. Us passengers were thrown on to the floor of the vehicle. He walked on and didn't apologize to any of us. We had to go to ask Sister Nurse for pills to ease our aches and pains. None of us realized the severity of back injuries.

THE FINAL STRETCH

Matt called Father Francis one time to ask permission to take me to see a movie. Father Francis and Sister Marcela trusted me and said yes. Matt arrived at the school one Saturday evening to take me to see the movie *The Odd Couple*. I liked the music and hummed along. Afterwards, we went to a restaurant for coffee, which seemed to be the popular thing to do. Matt brought me back to the school, proving himself a true gentleman. I was certain that students and staff were watching at every window. I felt giddy and grown up, and the coffee kept me awake all night.

In May, there was a big rodeo in north Kamloops. A friend from Merritt had relatives who were attending, and she asked me to join her. We got permission from Father Francis, and one of her uncles came to collect us. It was a dusty, noisy event with the usual offerings: bronc busting, calf roping, steer wrestling and such. After supper, it was time to go back to the school. No one wanted to drive us back, so we called a taxi. Two friends of the family, cowboys in tight blue jeans, offered to escort us in the cab. We didn't need escorting, especially from two guys who'd had too much to drink. What would Father Francis say? However, they couldn't be deterred. They tried their best to act like gentlemen, apologizing for their constant cussing, but their efforts were comical.

"Sorry, ladies. Pardon my French," one boy said, bowing and tipping his cowboy hat in earnest. "Don't mind us."

If we had spoken like them at school, we would have had our mouths washed out with soap. Halfway back to the school, they stopped the taxi to relieve themselves by the side of the road. The two cowboys paid for the taxi and off they went, leaving us to have a good laugh.

Close to my graduation date, Matt brought me a beautiful cedar root basket made by his Aunt Serafina. It was shaped like a round bowl with a lid; it was exquisite. My grandmother had intended to teach me how to make cedar root baskets one summer, but it hadn't panned out. We pulled roots from the ground under a cedar tree and cleaned them, but we didn't finish. I excitedly called Mom to tell her about Matt, his aunt and the basket.

"Oh, I know Serafina. Our grandmothers are first cousins," she explained, my heart sinking. "Yes, Serafina makes beautiful baskets. Make sure you hold on to that. She sells her baskets for a lot of money."

I recalled Mom speaking about her family travelling to Lytton to visit relatives long ago. Their idea of fun when they were kids was to go on a trip sitting on a wagon pulled by a team of horses and camping out along the way. Forty miles couldn't be covered in one day back then. Lots of excitement to visit other children, play games, have fun, share food together. Good memories. Mom liked to learn about medicine plants in different regions.

I treasured my basket but was sad to say goodbye to Matt, who was equally chagrined to learn that we didn't have a future together due to our newfound genetic proximity. I was embarrassed and didn't say another word about the discovery. I'm glad Mom didn't press the issue.

Soon, prom was upon us. Father Francis gave me fifty dollars to buy a dress in town. My sister Deanna sent me cash, and I purchased white sandals. I didn't have an escort for the prom now that Matt was out of the picture, so I invited a quiet young man who worked nearby, a former student who had graduated the year before. Everything set, we joined the other graduates at the prom. We looked the part but didn't seem to fit in. This just wasn't our world.

Some of my classmates invited us to their home in north Kamloops for a get-together. We joined them and visited for a while, making pleasant enough small talk. Graduation was an exciting time for all of us, but our plans weren't fully formulated yet and, beyond that, we didn't have much to talk about. So, we thanked our hosts for their hospitality, grateful they had reached out and made the effort to make us feel included. But we said our goodbyes knowing we'd probably not see each other again, fully expecting to go our separate ways.

GRADUATION — 1969

St. Ann's Academy outfitted us with white caps and gowns for the graduation ceremony. We posed for photos and received our certificates. That piece of paper signified success, hard work and determination; we hoped it would open doors to a better future and new opportunities. I was one of three graduates from the Indian residential school that evening; yet in grade eight, there were sixty-five of us. I wondered where my friends and schoolmates had gone.

Receiving a Dogwood Diploma with official high school transcripts would allow me to enter university for teacher training. Deanna had completed a teaching degree, and I wanted to follow in her footsteps. She encouraged me, promising that I wouldn't be forced to study the poetry of Byron and Keats.

My parents and a few of my siblings attended the graduation ceremony. They smiled broadly and showered me with gifts. I received a typewriter from Robert, a camera from Fred, a new watch from Mom, a new radio from Sarah and money from Deanna. I felt very important because everyone in my family worked hard for what little money they had. I could always count on their support; they taught me to celebrate all the milestones in our lives, and they recognized a job well done. People at the school rarely encouraged us, congratulated our successes or let us know in any way that we did a good job. Those words were missing. It was at this time I made a decision not to pray to God again, or go to church again. The religion and religious people at this school caused me to feel condemned to hell.

Dad had told me that when he attended Mission Residential School, "When the priests punished and whipped us, they meant to cripple us."

When Mom was whipped at school, she said she felt that Sister Malachi was intent on killing her.

I had graduated and felt happy about that, but like Mom and Dad I felt threatened and emotionally crippled.

Sister Marcela surprised us three grads with lovely jewelry boxes. She had enlisted all the girls to earn extra money by doing odd jobs for school staff and administrators—their efforts had taken place right under our noses. Looking into their faces, I hoped that when they graduated someone would honour their accomplishments. I didn't have any jewelry to put into the box, but I treasured it, nonetheless. That act of generosity helped to heal some of the wounds but not all, of the past twelve years. Sister Marcela mentioned that she hadn't seen me smile all year. I didn't reply. There was nothing more to say. I was finished there and free to move on.

On my last day at the school, I stood outside the building waiting for my ride home. I made sure to thank Father Francis for helping me throughout the years. He was the one person at school who made it possible for me to reach my goal. He had even written me a glowing letter of reference for a scholarship from the Kamloops Legion for children of veterans (though it ultimately went to a non-Native girl with higher marks). He had watched me grow from a silly little girl into a young lady.

Sister Margery, a snooty nun who never had a kind word for me, walked by. With her nose in the air and sneering, she asked me what I planned to do now that I had graduated.

"I want to be a teacher," I said.

"Hmph, you'll never make a teacher," she retorted and walked on.

With that one snide comment, my elation faded. My head hung down in shame and humiliation once again. It felt like I had been beat up; not physically, but mentally, emotionally and spiritually. That familiar numbness I had cultivated over the years to carry me through bad times returned. I felt I had no right to respond or speak up for myself. I had no rights at all. I should never have been born. I felt worthless and contemptible.

When Mom and Dad pulled up, I climbed into the back seat of their little Ford sedan, gaining my joy and confidence back at the sight of them. I'd left the prom dress hanging in the upstairs closet, thinking that another girl might find a use for it in future. I doubted I'd ever need it again. Being together with family was what I needed.

I never told my parents or anyone else about life at residential school—the years of scolding, shame and degradation—though they probably suspected it because of their own residential school experiences. They acted hopeful that things were better for me.

Passing by the primary school building I recognized my grades three and four classrooms, but not grades one or two. Suddenly the image of Sister Thomasa's raised arm with a thick leather strap came to mind. The two blank years fit into place. I recalled why the memories of my first two grades were missing.

"Do you remember me after I finished grade one?" I asked Mom.

"Yes."

"Do you remember me telling you I hated school and wanted to quit?"

"Yes," she said.

"What kind of a child was I back then?"

"You were quiet, not the lively kid who ran around noisily with your brother," she said.

I left it at that.

We were heading down the highway toward Joeyaska, and I didn't look back.

Xwikin nes wist. I am going home.

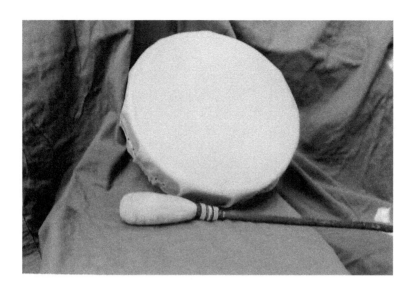

I go forward my confused mind swirling.
My wounded soul remains bruised.
I ignore the dagger in my heart.
It is time to seek kindness, beauty and truth.
I will go to the Medicine Tree.
I will go to the water.
I will sing my song and yemit, say my prayer.

ACKNOWLEDGEMENTS

Many thanks go to my good friend, sister and role model, Deanna, *Lalma*.

Thank you, Austin (*Hepelexqin*) and Fred (*Kayupa*) my brothers who are always ready to help.

My late siblings Shirley *Seepeetza* and brother Robert *Sesl qun*, and *Sarah Cul'culinek*, good teachers who taught me that laughter is medicine.

I am grateful to the late Mabel Joe who generously shared her teachings with me.

The late Sister Beverly Mitchell who broke the rule of assimilation and invited us to be part of reconciliation before we knew what those words meant.

The Gottfriedson family of the Kamloops Reserve for the loan of three beaded buckskin dresses in April 1968. A shining memory of my years at the residential school.

Thanks to Adam Bennet who gave me my first drum.

Kwuks chemxw.

HANDS LIFTED UP IN THANKS TO:

Carolee Dutchen and the prayer team at Redemption Church.

Shelley MacDonald who invited me to many, many schools.

The students in Vancouver schools who asked to hear my story.

Lori Sherritt Fleming who read my first rough draft and gave me hope.

Lindsay Tripp who read the second draft and introduced me to a publisher.

My nephew Ron Sterling who brings me fresh huckleberries in the autumn.

And my wonderful husband Wayne who lets me win at Scrabble.

A BRIEF HISTORY OF RESIDENTIAL SCHOOLS

Beginning with the Gradual Civilization Act of 1857, and the Indian Act of 1876 the Government of Canada intended to assimilate and subjugate First Nations because land was required for "progress". When chiefs lost and surrendered large tracts of land, education and schooling was listed as crucial in that exchange. 130 schools were built, Canadian law made it mandatory for children to be removed from families, languages, traditions and customs. Churches stepped in to carry out the education, regimentation and conversion of Indigenous children, and for decades subjected most of the children to shameful treatment including physical, mental, emotional and sexual abuse. Those in charge appeared to have no accountability for their actions.

More than 150,000 children were forced to attend, thousands died. Mass graves recently uncovered reveal that many children died of starvation, disease and murder, having been beaten to death as revealed by autopsies. Many children chose suicide, and most suffered in secret not knowing the truth about how or why they survived such an a dehumanizing system. On the whole, no one explained colonization, loss of land, legal rights or systemic racism. This resulted in pain, and unresolved, unspoken grief. Most of us staggered out of those brick buildings without a clue as to how to adapt or how to fit in to a modern world. How do victims indoctrinated with venomous messages of self hatred and self destruction and learn to become human beings and begin to heal? destruction become human and begin to heal?

Answer:

Our people were silenced. Canada now has an opportunity to practice inclusion and respect toward Indigenous people. Tackle and eliminate systemic racism. Become good listeners. Everyone has two ears, one to listen and one to hear. Colonization separated and isolated us (cultural genocide). When educational institutions step forward to include a true history of Canada, true reconciliation will take place. Reach out, make connections, correct what is wrong and make it right, make a positive difference!

For more information go to:

-Aboriginal Healing Foundation and the Legacy of Hope Foundation.
-Royal Commission on Aboriginal People's Report.
-Speaking Our Truth, A Journey of Reconciliation, Monique Gray Smith, Orca Publishers 2017.
-Truth and Reconciliation Commission.

https://www.cbc.ca/archives/topic/a-lost-heritage-canadas-residential-schools

https://www.orangeshirtday.org

https://www.cbc.ca/radio/secretlifeofcanada/teaching-guide-the-indian-act-1.5290134

Berger, Thomas R. A LONG AND TERRIBLE SHADOW: White values, native rights in the Americas since 1492. Douglas & McIntyre. 1999.

Milloy, John. The Story of a National Crime: An Appeal for Justice to the Indians of Canada.

Dr. Peter Henderson Bryce.

The Terrible Legacy of Duncan Campbell Scott.

WAYS OF HEALING

My parents and grandmother honored these traditional practices:

1. Sweat Lodge for cleansing and purification.
2. Yemit daily, pray. When washing your face, ask for cleansing from the past. It's a new day, a new beginning.
3. Daily request wisdom and strong thinking power. Proverbs 4:7 & 8 Seek wisdom.
4. Daily give thanks to the Creator. Find things to be grateful for and speak gratitude. Life is a gift to be a blessing to others.
5. Brush away negative energy such as sickness, anger, bitterness, insults, injury, loss with a fir branch or cedar bough at the water. An active brushing away such negativity and by asking the Creator to remove these from your life is a tangible action to promote letting go the bad, and requesting good replacements.
6. Dip in the water for cleansing, healing and purification. To be renewed from on high.
7. Smoke represents our prayers and good words rising to the Creator. Burn some dried sage, tobacco or sweetgrass and ask the Creator to cleanse your mind, eyes, ears, heart, mouth, spirit, soul and body so that all may go well with you.
8. The drum can be a voice to honor the Creator and our ancestors. The drumbeat is a heartbeat. A strong steady drumbeat combats sickness and disease.

9. Write a letter to the Creator to name those who harmed you, describe that mistreatment and ask for a peaceful solution. Tear up and/or burn that letter, let it all go by seeking to forgive others in order to begin anew.
10. Belief in, and maintaining communication with the Creator, the High and Holy Chief was and is key to finding healing and peace.

Zo zo eł chi – yia tlo: Stay strong and be well!

EPILOGUE

Ntle'kepmx elders prayed these words to the Creator at a place called *The Medicine Tree*. A tall pine tree on a hill south of Merritt. The wind whistled through withered branches as if whispering and singing answers to anyone willing to wait and listen:

"There are two roads.
Show me which road to take.
Do I go to the left? Do I go to the right?
Show me which road to take.
I will listen for the answer.
Sing the answer to me and I will sing to you."

Similar words can be found in the book of Jeremiah 6:16.

Ya-yeh told me our ancestors who passed away traveled to the stars and became Star People. Someday we will go to join them.
She told me to hold out my hands,
"Everything you have ever said and done is written on your hands.
You will stand in front of the Creator
And hold out your hands.
The Creator will read your hands.
Are you ready?"

Four of us selected for the Valentine's Dance 1969.

Bannock Recipe (*Sep'lil*)

11/2Cups (400 mL) all purpose flour
½ Cup (125 mL) whole wheat flour
1 Tbsp (15.0 mL) baking powder
1 tsp (5.0 mL) salt (or less)
1 Cup (250 mL) water
½ Cup (125 mL) canola oil for frying

Mix dry ingredients together in bowl.
Add the water stirring slowly.
Heat oil in a heavy frying pan on medium/low heat.
Divide the batter into five equal parts.
Gently pat each ball adding more flour and flatten.
Flatten to 5" (12 cm) let rest before frying.
Pierce center of bannock 1" (2 cm) with knife.
Fry 2 - 3 minutes on each side to golden brown.

Serve with blueberry jam!

Lightning Source UK Ltd.
Milton Keynes UK
UKHW052145071021
391777UK00012BA/2507